Contents

Peer Play

Age-Right Play

Playful Learning for Infants, Toddlers, and Preschoolers

by
Susan L. Lingo

Loveland, Colorado

This book is dedicated with love to my late
father who taught me that a child's smile is
worth a million rainbows!

Age-Right Play

CREDITS
Editors: Jody Brolsma and Beth Rowland Wolf
Senior Editor: Paul Woods
Chief Creative Officer: Joani Schultz
Copy Editor: Janis Sampson
Art Director: Lisa Chandler
Cover Art Director: Lisa Chandler
Designer: Diana Walters
Computer Graphic Artist: Ray Tollison
Illustrator: Joan Holub
Production Manager: Ann Marie Gordon

Unless otherwise noted, Scriptures quoted from The Youth Bible, New Century
Version, copyright © 1991 by Word Publishing, Dallas, Texas 75039. Used by
permission.

Library of Congress Cataloging-in-Publication Data
Lingo, Susan L.
        Age-right play / Susan L. Lingo.
                p.   cm.
        Includes index.
        ISBN 0-7644-2014-3
        1. Play. 2. Games. 3. Education, Preschool. I. Title.
LB1140.35.P55L55 1997
155.4'18—dc21   97-12084
                                                           CIP
10 9 8 7 6 5 4 3 2 1   06 05 04 03 02 01 00 99 98 97   AC
Printed in the United States of America.

Introduction

What is "child's play"?

Is it the time you played Hide-and-Seek with your cousins? pretended to teach Sunday school with your Susie Smart doll? built a ride-in racer with Dad? Or is it the memory of unencumbered delights, worry-free winsomeness,

> "**Being** with you will fill me with joy."
> PSALM 16:11B

and the time you spent discovering life? Whatever your definition of child's play, you might be surprised to find that behind the obvious delights of play-time hides a wealth of childhood learning.

Play helps children learn about themselves, others, and God's world around them. It's how children develop self-confidence and creativity and how they master many language and motor skills. Play is what kids "do." Producing as much social, physical, emotional, and experiential growth as adult jobs, play to a child is what work is to an adult—a worthwhile and necessary occupation.

> **The purpose of play is to have a good time. The outcome of play is intellectual, physical, emotional, and social development.**

All children engage in play—but all play isn't necessarily stage appropriate for all children. *Stage appropriate?* That's right! We hear many child psychologists and developmental specialists tout the need for age-appropriate activities and lessons in education—but play also needs to be geared toward stage appropriateness.

All children go through certain stages of physical, verbal, social, emotional, and cognitive development. We realize that children travel through these developmental stages on a continuum. The catch? These stages don't always correspond to specific chronological ages. You can think of the difference in this way: Age appropriateness is geared to *chronological age;* stage appropriateness is geared to *developmental stage.*

This means a four-year-old might possess the verbal development of a five-year-old but display the social development of a three-year-old. In some developmental areas this continuum shift makes little difference—but not in child's play. What happens if you urge a too-young child to share his or her toys with a playmate? Frustration, anger, and tears—and from the child as well! That's because very young children aren't developmentally *ready* to share toys or play socially with peers.

The key then to successful, confidence-building play is to offer young children *stage-appropriate* games and activities. And as we learn about children and their play, we can thank God for the wondrous ways that children develop. As the psalmist wrote, "I praise you because you made me in an amazing and wonderful way" (Psalm 139:14a). Keep reading to discover and develop a working knowledge of the four stages of play.

What are the four stages of play?

Basically, play patterns fit into four stages, with each stage occurring on a developmental continuum. Here are the four stages of play and a brief description of the play patterns and types of activities to expect in each stage.

Play Continuum

birth	2 years	3 years	4 years	5-6 years	7 years →	organized sports, team games, and adult leisure activities
Personal Play	Parallel Play	Partner Play	Peer Play			

STAGES 1 AND 2: Personal and Parallel Play

Personal and parallel play are closely related and will be covered in the same chapter. The difference between personal play and parallel play? Personal play is adult-initiated. It's a baby or very young child playing one-on-one with a loving adult or older sibling. Examples of personal play would be a young toddler and an adult playing This Little

Piggy or finding colors and objects in a Bible storybook.

Parallel play is one child playing beside another—both "doing their own thing"—but not interacting. Examples of parallel play include children sitting side by side, each putting together a different puzzle or building separate block towers.

STAGE 3: Partner Play

Partner play involves two and sometimes three children playing and interacting with each other. For example, two children "paving" roads in a sandbox and then sharing with each other the roads, their toy cars, and their imaginations.

STAGE 4: Peer Play

Peer play is associative play, or in simpler terms, group play. It's characterized by the child's ability to associate and communicate with a group of children and the increase in his or her ability to understand more organized "rules" for simple games and relays.

As you read *Age-Right Play*, you'll find that each chapter introduction further explains each developmental stage and how it relates to play. You'll be given the tools and information you need to offer stage-appropriate games and activities.

But before going on to the activities, there's another element of play that will be worthwhile to explore. In the preceding pages we've discussed stage appropriateness, which has to do with what a child is ready for developmentally—it corresponds to *how* children learn. But it's also important to understand play types. Play is also divided into four types that correspond to *what* children learn.

The four key play types are creative, spatial, conversational, and discovery. These play types can be found in each developmental stage. A brief description of each type follows.

Creative Play

Creative play engages a child's wondrous imagination and invites him or her to step into the realm of self-expression and exploration. It's play filled with whimsy and wonder, marvel and make-believe—in short, creative play is utterly "funciful"! Creative play utilizes crafts, building blocks, sculpting, felt boards with biblical characters, imaginary-friend play, role-playing, and Bible-costume play.

Spatial Play

In spatial play, children explore how the world moves and responds in relation to themselves, others, and their environment. Spatial play helps children see how far a ball rolls, how high they can jump, or what shapes are found in the world. Spatial play is more cognitive than creative play, which is emotive. Elements of spatial play include building blocks, playground play, large and fine motor skill games, Bible puzzles, number games, weights and scales, and cooking activities.

Conversational Play

"Where's your head? Find your nose.
Tickle your tummy—touch your toes."

Conversational play uses language as its foundation. Through the endless game-like "why's" to the more sophisticated "Let's pretend" games, conversational play helps children develop language and comprehension skills necessary for more advanced play and learning. Included in conversational play are games and activities that implement finger rhymes, Bible storytelling, action songs, choruses, poems, alphabet games, color identification, and more organized games with verbal rules.

Discovery Play

Discovery play is a natural extension for young children, allowing them to use their sense of curiosity and exploration to investigate the world. We can play with them as we discover together: "Lord, you have made many things; with your wisdom you made them all" (Psalm 104:24a).

In discovery play, children become budding scientists and explore cause and effect; how things are "put together"; what properties various substances, such as mud, possess; and how "tools," such as scissors, hammers, and screwdrivers, work. Discovery play items include "talking" and wind-up toys; tools; magnifying glasses; and the tactile elements: sand, mud, and water.

Age-Right Play

In this book, the chapters are organized around developmental stages of play, starting with games that are appropriate for babies. This will help you pick games that are right developmentally. Within each chapter, the games are identified by play type. This will help you choose games that develop particular skills or thought processes.

Play seldom falls neatly into one play type. When two young children are shoveling sand on the beach, they're engaged in creative play, discovery play, and probably a bit of conversational play—all revolving within the stage of parallel or partner play. To make your job easier and to find stage-appropriate games in a snap, use the Game Guide at the back of this book. It quickly identifies the stages and play types of each game and activity included in *Age-Right Play.*

Let the Play Begin!

In every parent, teacher, and child, there's an oasis of playfulness waiting to be tapped and tickled. For some, this playfulness comes through rough-and-tumble games, for others by building pretend skyscrapers or inventing imaginary friends.

Whatever the release of this wonderful playfulness, the outcome is delightful—and for a few precious moments, we become children with our children! Remember...

"The kingdom of God belongs to people who are like these children.' "
MARK 10:14B

Personal and Parallel Play

"Then Jesus took the children in his arms, put his hands on them, and blessed them."

MARK 10:16

Understanding the Stage

Great learning happens in one of the most unlikely places in your church—the nursery. As babies and toddlers engage the world and interact with nursery workers, they're taking in all kinds of information, and they're learning about sounds, facial expressions, emotions, and relationships with other people. You can enhance the learning by using the simple one-on-one games in this chapter.

"Play is as important for a baby's and toddler's normal growth and development—both physically and emotionally—as food, clean air, and sufficient sleep," says Dr. Michael B. Gothenburg, professor emeritus of pediatrics and psychology at the University of Washington School of Medicine.

Babies and children up to two years old *do* play, but need adults to stimulate many playtime activities. Waving rattles, playing This Little Piggy, and singing "Jesus Loves Me" all engage very young children in pleasant play and stimulate their social, physical, and cognitive learning skills.

Personal and parallel play, the first two stages of play, are two distinct but similar categories in the developmental stages of play. Both stages will be briefly discussed here, but the emphasis will be upon personal play which is the most distinctive of the two stages.

None of the games in this chapter are lengthy. And they're designed for easy use at home or at church—even when there's only one worker in the nursery. To use these games in a nursery setting, choose two or three games and set up any needed equipment in "stations" around the room. Then have the worker rotate among the children, taking two or three minutes to play a game with an individual child. With children who have moved into the parallel play stage, set up the games and encourage children to play the games. Have the worker engage each child individually in conversation about the game.

Personal Play

Personal play is characterized by adult-initiated games. Think of play as a circle in which children are occupied in entertaining activities and games. In personal play, babies and young two-year-olds become the focus of playtime and the center of their own circles of entertainment. If you picture the circle of personal play, the child would be alone and at the center—until an adult or older sibling enters and *initiates and stimulates* play.

To illustrate the importance of adult-initiated games, picture a pile of blocks in the young child's circle of entertainment. The blocks would be ignored or simply held and observed—but not actually played with. Babies lack the cognition, imagination, and motor skills needed to invent their own play activities. In essence, then, adults teach babies and very young children *how* to play.

Personal play is the shortest stage of play and generates the most intense bonding. Relying on adults for their basic physical needs, babies and very young toddlers also depend on loving caregivers for cognitive stimulation and relaxation—both of which are essential for human well-being. Personal play creates an emotional, psychological, and cognitive bond between the child and adult "playmate." And for a few short months, this stage of development is as important as cuddling, nurturing, and caring for a child.

Games and activities common in personal play include simple finger rhymes and games, such as Peekaboo and Patty-Cake; soft lullabies, such as "Away in a Manger"; mirror play; exploring bodies and facial expressions; and sensory-type games, such as pounding on pots and pans, ringing Christmas bells, and looking at bright Bible storybooks.

Parallel Play

Parallel play is the next stage of development. When children enter this stage, they've learned to play by themselves. The fascinating aspect of this stage is a child's proximity to other children.

Imagine two parallel lines: side by side, not touching, each line in its own separate space. Now imagine two very young children playing with building blocks: side by side, not touching, each in his or her own separate space. This is parallel play.

In simple terms, parallel play involves children playing next to each other without physical interaction. In this stage, a child first notices and tolerates a peer in his or her circle of entertainment. Too immature to have invited the playmate and too curious to send him or her away, a child engaged in parallel play tolerates another child with an easy-going style as long as toys and personal space aren't threatened.

Children will play next to each other far sooner than they will play with others or share their toys with others. Don't push the idea of sharing at this stage. As young children become aware of the existence of things, they become intensely possessive. Children naturally reason that if they see something they desire, that it automatically becomes theirs. Gently introduce the concept of sharing with statements such as "It makes God happy when we share," "Look how happy it made Lorie when you shared the truck with her," or "God likes it when we play nicely with each other."

Parallel play can be seen in any early childhood classroom. The moment you step through the door, you'll probably see many children playing—but not necessarily with each other. Does this mean, then, that parallel play involves no interaction between children? Not at all! Children involved in parallel play are keenly aware of what their "neighbors" are doing—how they're using their toys, what sounds they're making, and how their bodies are moving. Imitation almost becomes a play form itself as children try out what their neighbors are doing. "Can I make that sound?" "Can I pile my blocks like that?" "Can I crawl that way?"

Children learn a great deal from each other during parallel play even though there is an absence of physical interaction—which presents a peculiar challenge. Since there's a lack of interaction between children, it's difficult to present specific games and activities geared to parallel play. It's best to set up play situations that encourage children to comfortably play beside each other in nonthreatening ways, such as providing each child his or her own pile of blocks or toys.

The following games and activities all revolve around stages of personal and parallel play and will stimulate the child's sense of creativity, spatial concepts, conversation, and discovery. Each activity is based on one of the four play types discussed in the book's introduction. You'll also find a stated learning goal and valuable "Play Pointers" that offer tips and insights into child development.

Have fun playing and sharing the delights of simple learning fun!

Won't you stop to play awhile?
I may be small, but I can smile!
Jesus loves me—this I know—
Because you smiled and told me so!

The Games

Glad Doggie, Sad Doggie
Conversational

Developmental Skill:
The child will learn about EMOTIONS.

Simple Supplies:
You'll need two paper plates: one with a happy face and one with a sad face. For a fun touch, tape floppy paper ears on the paper plate faces.

Cuddle with a child, and place the happy and sad paper plates beside you. Hold up the happy face and say: **Here's Glad Doggie. Can you smile like Glad Doggie?** Smile at the child, and encourage him or her to smile with you. Then say: **How does Glad Doggie bark?** Bark a few happy woofs. Then repeat the process for Sad Doggie. Explain to children that God gave us many feelings. Sometimes we feel happy and other times we feel angry or sleepy or silly. When the child is familiar with "glad" and "sad," hold the Glad Doggie paper plate, and repeat the following rhyme. Encourage the child to imitate your actions.

Glad Doggie. *(Smile.)*
Sad Doggie. *(Look sad.)*
Nice Doggie. *(Pat the Glad Doggie.)*
Naughty Doggie. *(Shake your finger.)*
Weepy Doggie. *(Wipe away pretend tears.)*
Sleepy Doggie. *(Pretend to sleep.)*
Wake up! *(Open your eyes.)*
Woof, woof, woof, doggie! *(Bark happily.)*

Play Pointer
Even babies enjoy the playful sounds and rhythms of rhyming words. The key to offering rhymes to young children is in repetition. Hearing a familiar rhyme gives security to little ones and before you know it, the child will be repeating the rhyme and actions with you.

For another fun twist, encourage the child to point to the correct paper plate doggie faces as you say "glad" or "sad." Repeat the rhyme at bedtime or nap time and stop after saying, "Sleepy Doggie." Then say, "Hush, hushaby."

Mirror, Mirror

Discovery

Developmental Skill:
The child will learn about BODY AWARENESS.

Simple Supplies:
You'll need a blanket and a hand-held mirror or a full-length mirror.

Spread a blanket on the floor, and set out the mirror. If you have a light-weight full-length mirror, prop it up on the floor lengthwise using books or chairs. Curl up on the floor with a child; be sure you can see your reflections in the mirror.

Look in the mirror and say: **Oh! Who's in the mirror? Who's face do I see? That's** (child's name). **Can you see me? I can see** (child's name). **I can see your nose.** Point directly to the child's nose. **I can see your ears.** Point to the child's ears. **I can see your hair.** Point to the child's hair. Continue in this way several more times. Then give a slight twist to the game by asking: **Can you point to your nose? Can you point to your ears?** And so on.

Children will love this affirming rhyme especially about them. Say the child's name and point to his or her facial features as you repeat the following rhyme.

> **Who's in the mirror? Do I have a clue?**
> **That's** (name)**'s** (nose)**, and** (name)**'s** (hair)—
> **And God loves you!**

Play Pointer

Mirrors are inexpensive and provide many hours of discovery fun. Check into new break-proof Mylar mirrors that attach to the sides of a playpen or wall. Young children will entertain themselves and begin to initiate their own play with these safe mirrors.

Here are a few other mirror activities to use with very young children.

● Play Peekaboo by holding a mirror up to the child's face and saying "peekaboo," then hiding the mirror and saying, "Where's (child's name)?"

● Simply lie in front of a full-length mirror and make funny faces. Create different imitative movements by touching your toes, bending your knees, and putting your legs in the air and wiggling your feet.

● Balance a full-length mirror on two chairs, and lie under the mirror for a different view. Be sure the child doesn't kick or knock the mirror off the chairs.

Clackety Cups

Spatial

Developmental Skill:
The child will learn STACKING SKILLS.

Simple Supplies:
You'll need a blanket and three or more plastic tumblers.

> ### Play Pointer
> Plastic tumblers are wonderful "play equipment"—safe and inexpensive! Look for dollar-day sales and pick up a colorful dozen.

Spread a blanket on the floor, and set out the plastic tumblers. If the child is a baby, hold him or her in your lap. Clap together the open ends of two plastic tumblers. Say: **Clack-clack-clackety-clack! Can you make the cups go clackety-clack?** Let the child bang two tumblers together. Then repeat the rhyme and add: **Stack-stack-stackety-stack.** Place one tumbler inside another as you say the rhyme. Invite the child to stack the cups, then pull them apart. Continue the clackety-clack, stackety-stack game for a few repetitions.

Spread the cups on the floor, and demonstrate how to stack the tumblers upside down, bottom to bottom in pairs, and side by side. Then encourage the child to stack the cups in any way he or she desires as you say, "Stack-stack, stackety-stack." For a variation, help the child stack cups by alternating turns. Your little one will begin to learn about partner play and enjoy a bit of happy teamwork.

Cereal Sorter

Spatial

Developmental Skill:
The child will learn about SORTING SHAPES.

Simple Supplies:
You'll need a bedsheet; a bowl; and a variety of cereal shapes and colors, such as fruity loops, oat loops, alphabet cereal, and cereal squares.

Pour the cereal into a large bowl, and spread a clean bedsheet on the floor. Place the bowl of cereal in the center of the sheet, and sit with a child by the bowl. Pull out cereal loops, and encourage the child to find one that is the same.

When a match is made, say "match-match." Invite the child to select a cereal bit, then you find one that matches and say "match-match." Repeat the match-match activity until a match of each type of cereal has been made. Then say: **Look! We made match-match pairs. Let's put all the match-matches into one pile.** Help the child sort the cereal bits into their correct piles.

Play Pointer

By saying the words "match-match," the child will begin to understand what it means when two or more things are the same. When children are a bit older, they'll be able to match-match colors, shapes, and numbers.

When all or most of the cereal bits are sorted, say: **Good job! That was fun. Now let's taste the yummy cereal. I'll eat a piece of cereal, and you can eat one just like it.** Eat a piece of cereal, then let the child choose and nibble the same kind of cereal.

Here are a few game variations to play with the child.

● Place a simple cereal pattern in a line. Use three or four pieces of cereal, then encourage the child to make a row just like it below your cereal bits.

● Put a small pile of various cereal loops in front of the child. Pull a piece of cereal from the bowl, and have the child find a piece in his or her pile that makes a "match-match."

● Let the child use a plastic spoon to scoop cereal bits into a bowl or a small cup.

One, Two, Peekaboo!
Spatial

Developmental Skill:
The child will learn about COUNTING.

Simple Supplies:
none

This fun little game includes an important beginning number activity. Cuddle a child on your lap and repeat the following rhyme and actions.

> **One, two** *(cover each eye as you count)*,
> **Peekaboo!** *(Peek through your fingers.)*
> **One, two** *(uncover each eye as you count)*,
> **I see you!** *(Point to the child's tummy.)*

Play Pointer

Simple counting rhymes help young children begin to memorize number sequence. Finger rhymes are especially effective since they offer children a concrete visual of counting.

Repeat the action rhyme until the child begins to cover his or her eyes with you. Now repeat the rhyme by holding your hands up to the child's eyes, and yet again by holding the child's hands up to your eyes. If the child is a middle two, hold up fingers as you count in the following rhyme. Encourage the child to join in the rhyme and shaking hands.

One, two *(hold up one finger at a time),*
I see you! *(Point to the child's tummy.)*
One, two *(hold up one finger at a time),*
How do you do? *(Shake hands with the child.)*

As you play this rhyme game, tell your child that God brought the animals "one, two" to the ark. Explain that God loved the animals he made and wanted to save them from the big flood. End with the following "One, Two" animal rhyme.

One, two,
I see who?
Elephants and kangaroos!

Surprise Purse

Conversational

Developmental Skill:
The child will learn about the element of SURPRISE.

Simple Supplies:
You'll need an old purse or large bag containing a variety of items, such as keys, a billfold, a pocket mirror, a comb, tissues, small toy animals, blocks, a small picture book, stuffed animal, and an apple.

Place the items in the purse or bag. Sit on the floor with a child, and set the purse in front of you. Say: **Oh, what is this? It's a surprise purse, and there are so many surprises inside! What do you think is in the purse?** Take a quick peek inside and act surprised. Make exclamations, such as "Oooo!" "Oh my!" and "Ahhh!"

Then say: **Would you like to peek in the purse, too? What can you find?** Invite the child to pull one item at a time out of the purse. Find interesting things to say about each item, such as "These keys start the car...vrooom, vrooom!" or "Apples are yummy. Would you like a bite?" If the child is a bit older, encourage him or her to tell something about each item.

After the purse is empty, try one or more of the following ideas.

- Count the items as you place them back in the purse.
- Play the game Can You Find? by asking, "Can you find the keys?"

"Can you find the comb?"

● Let the child pack the purse, then take a make-believe trip to the "toy store" (a play area). Invite the child to pick out a toy, then "pay" for it with something in the purse. Take the toy back to your starting place.

● Pack the purse with "natural" items, such as a stone, a twig, a flower, a piece of fruit, and a handful of grass in a plastic bag. Discover God's creation with the child by asking, "What did God make?" before the child takes an item out of the bag.

Bunny in the House

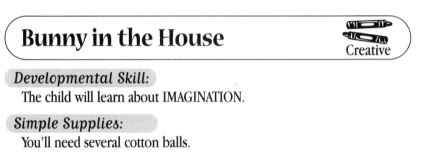

Creative

Developmental Skill:
The child will learn about IMAGINATION.

Simple Supplies:
You'll need several cotton balls.

Place a cotton ball in the palm of one hand. Say: **Here's a pretend bunny. He's so soft. God wants us to be kind to the animals he made. Would you like to pat the bunny?** Let the child pat the make-believe bunny. Then slightly close your hand, partially hiding the bunny. Say: **Oh, the bunny's in his little house. Come out, little bunny!** Repeat the following rhyme using the cotton ball bunny.

Little bunny in your house (*peek inside your hand*),

It's such a sunny day.

Come out now, little bunny (*shake your finger at the bunny*),

So we can hop and play! (*Open and shake your hand so the bunny "hops."*)

> ### Play Pointer
> Finger and action rhymes are great for little ones and help develop their imagination, fine motor skills, and vocabulary.

Repeat the rhyme a few times, and let the child hold the bunny as you say the words. Then say: **God made real bunnies. But we can be pretend bunnies. Let's hop and play.** Encourage the child to hold a cotton ball and hop like a bunny. Then place several cotton balls around the room in plain sight, and have the child join you on a "bunny hop" safari. Hop around the room collecting fluffy bunnies, then return to your starting place. Older children will enjoy counting the bunnies to end game time.

End by suggesting other animals God made and imitating their actions and sounds.

Roly-Ball

Spatial

Developmental Skill:
The child will learn large MOTOR SKILLS.

Simple Supplies:
You'll need a large ball.

Sit on the floor with your feet touching the child's feet. Roll the ball between your legs to the child as you say: **Roly-ball, roll.** Encourage the child to roll the ball back to you, and again say: **Roly-ball, roll.**

Very young children will be pleased with this simple game and may play Roly-Ball for some time before tiring. Next, try handing the ball to the child and saying, "Pass-a-ball, pass." For another twist, add a second ball to your game. Here are a few more variations for children who are a bit older.

● Stand up and play Bouncy-Ball in the same way as Roly-Ball.

● Set a few plastic tumblers in front of a wall. Let the child roll the ball and knock over the tumblers. Encourage the child to say "roly-ball" as he or she rolls the ball and "Ka-boom!" when a cup is knocked over. Let the child set the cups upright again.

What's That?

Conversational

Developmental Skill:
The child will learn IDENTIFICATION.

Simple Supplies:
You'll need a variety of toy animals. Small plastic animals or soft stuffed animals work equally well.

Very young children enjoy this game of identification and silly noises. Line the animals up in front of you and the child. Point to an animal and ask: **What's that?** Whatever his or her answer, reply: **That's a** (animal name). **God made** (animal name)**s.** Continue until all the animals have been identified. Repeat animal names the child may not know.

Play Pointer
Young children gain a sense of accomplishment and pride when they're able to correctly identify objects and pictures. Be sure to affirm the child's efforts and offer identification games often.

Explain that God made all the animals and told Adam to give the animals names such as "elephant," "lion," and "horse." Then put a fun twist on the game by pointing to an animal and asking: **What does the** (animal name) **say?** Imitate the appropriate animal sound, and encourage the child to follow.

Another way to play, is to make an animal noise and ask: **Who says oink-oink?** Then hold up the animal and say: **The pig says oink-oink. God made pigs.**

Identification games are easy to play and are loads of fun for little ones. Have children try to identify foods; pictures of people; and cars, trucks, boats, and other vehicles.

Rum-Sum-Sum

Creative

Developmental Skill:
The child will learn about RHYTHM AND RHYME.

Simple Supplies:
You'll need several plastic spoons and metal pots.

This simple, rhythmic rhyme from a favorite Moroccan chant is as fun to hear as it is to act out! Place the pots and spoons on the floor in front of you and the child. Say: **We love God soooo much! Let's tell God how much we love him with a special song!** Repeat the following rhyme several times in a lilting, lively manner.

A rum-sum-sum.
A rum-sum-sum.
Guli, guli, guli—
God is love!

Play Pointer

Don't worry if young children can't tap in time to a tune—they're not ready for that advanced skill. Smile! Young children derive great joy from making loud rhythmic noises—even if your ears don't.

Now repeat the rhyme as you clap in rhythm to the words. Encourage the child to clap with you—but don't expect him or her to clap on the appropriate beats. Just let the child enjoy the fun sounds of the words and the joy of clapping.

After a few repetitions, pick up a plastic spoon and bang on the pots as you repeat the words to the rhyme. For rhythm variations, clack together two plastic spoons, tap on your tummy, or rap on the pots with your fingers.

Encourage the child to create different ways to make sounds. You may wish to set out plastic containers, metal spoons, and pot lids for a unique rhythm section to praise God.

Oopsie-Dropsie

Spatial

Developmental Skill:
The child will learn about SIZES.

Simple Supplies:
You'll need several toys and cardboard tubes in various diameters and lengths. Use empty wrapping paper tubes or make your own tubes from poster board.

Set out the empty tubes and a selection of small and large toys. Be sure many of the toys and objects will slide through some of the tubes. Pick up a small toy and paper tube. Let the toy fall through the tube as you say, "Dropsie!" Then repeat the process with a different toy and tube. Each time the toy falls through the tube say, "Dropsie!" If a toy is too large for a tube say, "Oopsie, too big!" Encourage the child to experiment with different toys and tubes to see which toys will drop and which are too large.

> ### Play Pointer
> Even simple games like Oopsie-Dropsie provide great learning. This game helps young children develop visual tracking, understand simple cause-and-effect concepts, and determine size relationships.

Pick up a long tube and a short tube. Say: **Here's a big, long tube. Here's a small, short tube.** Help the child choose two different tubes. Then ask: **Which tube is bigger?** and **Which tube is smaller?** Return the tubes to the pile, and play "big and small" again.

Here are a few other games and activities using paper tubes.

● Let older toddlers decorate the tubes with crayons, stickers, and washable markers.

● Tape wax paper on one end of a paper tube, and let the child hum through the other end like a kazoo.

● Tape a length of yarn to one end of a paper tube, and let your little one "drive the train," "walk the doggie," or "pull the wagon."

Pudding Painting

Creative

Developmental Skill:

The child will learn about CREATIVITY.

Simple Supplies:

You'll need a tray or smooth table, a spoon, prepared chocolate pudding, plain paper, and damp paper towels.

Clean a tray or smooth table. You may wish to slip an old, short-sleeved shirt on the child, and place newspapers on the floor under his or her chair. Scoop a spoonful of pudding directly onto the tray, then encourage the child to move the pudding around the surface with his or her fingers and hands. Show the child how to make wavy lines, squiggles, circles, and whatever else your imagination holds. Tell the child that God gives us the gift of being able to make things such as lines and squiggles and big round O's.

Add more pudding, and turn the little one loose in his or her creativity. Affirm designs with comments such as "What a pretty picture you made" or "Isn't it fun to make shapes?" When the child is happy with a particular design, carefully lay a sheet of paper over the design and lightly rub your hands over the paper. Slowly lift the paper from the tray, and you'll have a print of the design to hang once it's dry. Then simply spoon more pudding onto the tray, and let the child begin a new picture.

Play Pointer

Self-expression without judgment is a keystone in helping children develop autonomy and self-worth. Offer your little ones opportunities to freely create, and affirm their efforts by displaying their artwork prominently.

Play Pointer

Painting with pudding is a valuable sensory experience for young children—they'll explore the touch, smell, and possibly even the taste of the pudding while they create. But if your children are tempted to play with their food at mealtime, explain that playtime is different from mealtime and that it's inappropriate to play with food at mealtime.

Use the damp paper towels for sticky hands clean-up. After the child's picture has dried, encourage him or her to tell you about the design. Be sure to proudly display the child's artwork so that you both see it often.

● Develop an older child's awareness of his or her senses. You can ask, "How does the pudding feel? Is it hot or cold? smooth or lumpy?" "How does the pudding smell? Is it sweet or spicy?" "How does the pudding sound? Can you make it 'squish' in your hand?" "How does the pudding taste? Is it vanilla or chocolate? sweet or sour?" and "What color is the pudding? dark or light?"

Little Fishy

Spatial

Developmental Skill:
The child will learn COUNTING.

Simple Supplies:
You'll need paper fish, tape, and string or yarn. Make festive fish by gluing bright wrapping paper to cardboard, then cutting out simple fish shapes. Tape a twelve-inch piece of string or yarn to each fish.

Place the paper fish on the floor beside you and the child. Say: **Look at the pretty fish. Which one do you like?** Let the child choose a fish to hold. Say: **Many people in the Bible were fishermen. They caught yummy fish to eat. Jesus even helped his friends catch fish. Let's learn a rhyme about catching fish.** Then hold up a clenched hand and repeat this favorite rhyme as you undo your fingers as little "fish." Repeat the rhyme several times.

> ### Play Pointer
> Look for fun ways to extend simple playtimes. Working numbers, letters, and colors into activities adds to the fun and challenge for young children.

One, two, three, four, five. *(Undo your fingers one at a time.)*
I caught a little fish alive. *(Make your hand "swim" back and forth.)*
Six, seven, eight, nine, ten. *(Undo the fingers on your other fist.)*
Then I let him go again! *(Make your hand "swim" back and forth.)*

Encourage the child to do the actions with you. Go slowly at first, and soon the child will get "in the swim." Then stand up and say the rhyme as you "reel" in your paper fish and pull it around the room.

Older toddlers will enjoy these fun variations.
- Pointing to and identifying colors on each paper fish.
- Counting the fish with the rhyme, especially if you have ten of them.
- Taping the ends of the fish-strings to a clothes hanger and suspending the fish from a window or light fixture as a mobile.
- Nibbling fish-shaped crackers as you repeat the little fishy rhyme.

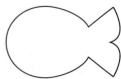

Picture Boxes

Conversational

Developmental Skill:
The child will learn about EXPRESSION.

Simple Supplies:
You'll need stickers; tape; and magazine pictures of animals, people, foods, and objects. You'll also need a shoe box or other small box.

Place the tape and box on the floor. Scatter the pictures beside you and the child. Let the child choose a picture, and encourage him or her to tell you about the picture. Or ask questions to stimulate the child's responses. Use questions such as "Where's the picture of the cake? What kind of cake do you think it is?" or "Do you see a fun toy? Why do you like that toy?" or "Can you find a red sticker? What other things are red?" After you've visited about the pictures and stickers, help the child create a picture box by taping magazine pictures and placing stickers on the sides of the shoe box.

Play Pointer

Pictures are wonderful tools that stimulate a child's imagination and verbal expression. Encourage the child to tell you about pictures he or she enjoys and to find objects and colors within the pictures.

When the box is finished, cuddle the child on your lap and talk more about the pictures and what you see on the box. You might enjoy making up stories about the pictures on the box. When playtime is finished, let the child set the picture box beside the bed to look at when waking up from naps.

In and Out of the Mountains

Spatial

Developmental Skill:
The child will learn large MOTOR SKILLS.

Simple Supplies:
You'll need a variety of medium and large boxes with the end flaps removed. Be sure the boxes are large enough to crawl in and through.

Place the boxes in the center of your play area. If you're short on boxes, place chairs or a table in the play area and cover them with old bedsheets and blankets to make "mountains."

Say: **God made everything in our world. God is so great, he even made the big, tall mountains. The Bible tells us that God made the mountains by his strength** (Psalm 65:6). Show the pretend mountains to the child and explain that he or she can crawl in and out, and around and under the mountains. If there's room, join the child in a crawl through the mountains. Then sing the following words to the tune of "The Bear Went Over the Mountain" as the child moves in and out and around the mountains.

In and out of the mountains,
In and out of the mountains,
In and out of the mountains—
Watch me creep along.

You can also show the child how to roll, crawl, or scooch around the mountains as you sing.

Encourage the child to pile the mountains in different configurations, then tumble the mountains and begin again. If you have older toddlers, provide brown and black washable markers, and invite them to color the mountains. You may even wish to tape cotton ball

Play Pointer

Boxes provide hours of creative fun for young children. Encourage little ones to turn boxes into cars, trucks, boats, houses, or screaming fire engines—the fun is endless!

"snow" or "clouds" to the sides of the mountains. If you're using a covered table, invite the child to come inside for a "mountain tea party." Serve apple juice and graham cracker "stones" for a tasty treat.

Shape Collage

Spatial

Developmental Skill:

The child will learn about SHAPES.

Simple Supplies:

You'll need a sheet of plain paper and a glue stick. You'll also need shapes cut from a variety of papers, such as aluminum foil, construction paper, wallpaper, gift wrap, and sandpaper.

Decide on a shape you want the child to become familiar with, such as a circle, triangle, or square. Cut several sizes of one shape from various kinds of paper. Scatter the shapes on a table, and set out the glue stick and sheet of paper. Hold up a shape, and tell the child the name of the shape and something about it. For example, if you're working with triangles say, "A triangle looks like a mountain God made." Or say, "A circle looks like the sun God made."

Then say: **Let's make a picture with shapes. I'll put glue on the (shape), and you stick it on the paper.** Put glue on the back of a shape, and let the child stick it to the paper. Then ask the child to choose another triangle he or she especially likes. Glue that shape to the paper. As you work, make comments about the way certain paper shapes feel, look, and shine. Continue until all the shapes have been added to the picture. Then hang the child's shape collage in a spot where it's sure to be noticed.

● Expand the learning by looking for that shape throughout the rest of the day. Encourage the child to be on "shape patrol" and point out all of the shapes he or she sees. For example, the child might point out a traffic sign that is a large triangle or crackers that are shaped like little circles.

Pretty Petunia

Discovery

Developmental Skill:
The child will learn about NATURE.

Simple Supplies:
You'll need several real flowers. Be sure the flowers have small leaves on the stems.

Let the child explore the flowers you have set out. Encourage the child to hold the flowers and smell them. Identify the petals, leaves, stem, and where the roots hold the flower tightly in the ground. Point out the color of the petals, the shape of the leaves, and how the stem holds the flower tall.

Say: **God made flowers to make our world beautiful. The Bible tells us that God made and clothes the lilies of the fields. That means that God makes the flowers beautiful and cares for them.** Then ask the child these simple questions about the flower.
● **Where are the pretty petals?**
● **Where are the small green leaves?**

- What color is the flower?
- Where is the tall stem?

If the child is very young, hand the flowers back and forth like small bouquets, and practice saying, "Thank you!" If the child is a bit older, repeat the following action rhyme and encourage the child to do the motions as you say the words.

Here are my petals, pretty and bright. *(Fluff out your hair.)*
Here is my stem, straight and tall. *(Stand straight and tall.)*
Here are the roots that hold me so tight. *(Wiggle your feet.)*
Here are my leaves, green and small. *(Wave your hands slightly.)*
God made flowers—one and all! *(Clap your hands.)*

I See a Cat

Creative

Developmental Skill:
The child will learn about ANIMALS.

Simple Supplies:
You'll need a book with colorful pictures of animals.

Cuddle with a child, and read a picture book together. Then find animal pictures, colors, and other objects. Ask the child to point out his or her favorite animal and ask: **What does a** (animal name) **say?** Imitate the sound that animal makes. Then tell the child you can play a fun animal game. Repeat the following rhyme about a cat, and encourage the child to fill in the animal sounds and find the animal's illustration in a picture book.

I see a cat.
What does it say?
"Meow, meow, meow!"
All night and day!
God made cats
To run and play!

Use the rhyme to continue play with other simple animal names and sounds. Here are a few extra-fun suggestions if the child is a bit older.

- Invite the child to walk, hop, or "swim" like the animals in the pictures.
- Pick an "Animal for the Day" and post its picture on the wall. Tell the child that whenever you say the animal's name that day, he or she can make that animal's noises.
- Look through a Bible storybook, and identify all the animals God made.

Little Echo

Conversational

Developmental Skill:
The child will learn to pronounce new WORDS.

Simple Supplies:
none

Cuddle a child on your lap. Say: **Let's play a new game. I'll say words, and you say them back. But if I say "clap," then you clap your hands instead of repeating my word. Ready?** Point to the child's tummy and say "tummy." Pause for the child to repeat the word "tummy." Say: **God made your tummy.**

Then point to the child's elbow and say "elbow." Again, pause for the child to repeat the word. Say: **God made your elbow.**

Say: **Clap** and wait for the child to clap his or her hands. Use "new" words such as "forehead," "thigh," "eyebrow," "kneecap," "shoulder," and "wrist." If the child is a bit older, invite him or her to tell words for you to repeat.

Play Pointer
Young children love the sounds of "new" words—and they enjoy the challenge of repeating the sounds. Though most young children won't dramatically increase their working vocabularies from these word games, their pronunciation and listening skills are being developed.

Copycat Ring-a-Ding

Creative

Developmental Skill:
The child will learn about simple RHYTHM.

Simple Supplies:
You'll need two strings of jingle bells. Purchase six to eight large jingle bells at a craft store, and string them on two eight-inch pieces of string, yarn, ribbon, or elastic thread.

Find a cozy corner to share with a child, and hand him or her a string of jingle bells. Take a few moments just to shake and jingle the bells and delight in the sweet sounds. Then tell the child you'll shake your bells and he or she can be a "copycat" and shake the bells the same way. Begin by giving the bells one short shake. Next, give them two short shakes. Then shake one time followed by two quick shakes. Each time, wait for the child to copy your actions.

Keep the patterns very simple—no more than three rings in a sequence. After a few turns, let the child be the "ringleader," and you be the copycat. End playtime by singing "Jingle Bells" while shaking your jingle bell strings. Then put the strings out of reach of the child to prevent any choking hazard. Assure the child that you'll play with the jingle bells soon—then be sure you do!

Play Pointer

Clapping, tapping, stomping, and clucking your tongue are great ways to engage young children in lively rhythms.

Picture Bags

Spatial

Developmental Skill:
The child will learn SORTING.

Simple Supplies:
You'll need index cards; paper lunch sacks; and several categories of stickers, such as animals, cars, flowers, robots, or geometric shapes. Place one of each category of sticker on a paper sack and the rest of the stickers on halves of index cards. Be sure there's one sticker per card half.

Set the sacks with the pictures facing the child and the picture cards in easy reach. If you're using this activity as parallel play, be sure each child has at least two sacks and a stack of picture cards. Show the child how to "match-match" the picture cards to the appropriate sacks and drop in the cards. Continue until all of the picture cards have been sorted into the correct sacks.

Then ask the child to draw out a card and tell something about the picture. For example, if a shape is drawn, have the child tell what shape and color it is. If an animal picture is chosen, have the child tell what animal it is and make the appropriate animal noises.

If the child is a bit older, spread the cards on

Play Pointer

Picture cards are simple to make and great take-along fun for trips and travels. Young children never tire of looking at colorful stickers and will delight in seeing their favorites again and again.

the floor face down and have him or her turn up two cards at a time. When matching cards are found, move them to the side. If matching cards aren't found, turn them face down again. Take turns turning over cards and making pairs. When a pair is made, clap and cheer.

Keep the picture cards in the sacks, and pull this game out often. Try the following variations using the sacks and cards.

Play Pointer

Use animal cards and explain how God brought the animals to the ark in pairs. Then match pairs of animal pictures.

● Line up the sacks. Have the child stand over them and drop cards into the sacks for a simple game of skill.

● Use the picture cards to tell stories. Place the cards on the floor as you tell your tale.

● Sort the cards into pairs, and put one card of each pair around the room in plain sight. Hand the child one picture at a time, and encourage him or her to go on a "picture card" safari and find the matching picture and bring it to you. Continue until all the cards have been found.

Box Walk

Creative

Developmental Skill:
The child will learn about IMAGINATION.

Simple Supplies:
You'll need a small box for each child, crayons, tape, yarn, a glue stick, and cotton balls.

Set out the craft materials and the boxes. If you're using this activity as parallel play, be sure each child has a box to decorate.

Say: **God made everything in our world, and everything God made is good. The Bible tells us that "God looked at everything he had made, and it was very good"** (Genesis 1:31a). **Let's have fun creating something, too.** Invite children to turn the box into a make-believe animal by decorating it with the craft supplies. Show children how to use crayons to make facial features and cotton balls for soft ears, puffy tails, or fuzzy tufts of fur. As each child works, make affirming comments, such as "What a cute little animal friend you're making" and "I like how you

Play Pointer

Creating pretend animals is a favorite activity for little ones. Make the animals from paper, paper cups, clay or modeling dough, or even old socks. Make-believe creatures stimulate imagination and conversation in young children.

made your animal's ears." Encourage the child to tell you about his or her animal as it's being made and to make up a name for the new "friend."

When the box animal is complete, tape a two-foot length of yarn to the box for a "leash." Let the child take his or her animal on a "walking tour" around the room. Add music for a fun touch, and tell the child to march, hop, walk, and tiptoe as he or she leads the box pet. If this is a parallel play activity, encourage children to let their pets "touch noses" and say "hello."

Leader of the Band Batons

Creative

Developmental Skill:
The child will learn about MUSIC.

Simple Supplies:
You'll need washable markers, tape, crayons, colored gift wrap or aluminum foil, and paint stir sticks available at no cost from most hardware stores. You'll also need lively praise music to march to.

This marching activity is a good one to use for parallel play. Before this activity, cut gift wrap or aluminum foil into long strips. Set out the paper strips, markers, crayons, and tape.

Hand the child a paint stir stick, and take one for yourself. Join with the child in decorating the paint sticks using colorful markers and crayons. Then tape several paper strips at one end of each stick for streamers. Hold the other end of the stick or "baton," and wave the stick in the air. Say: **Let's pretend we're leading a marching band that's praising God. We can march and wave our pretty batons in time to the music.** Start the music, and join the child in marching and waving the batons.

When the music is ended, try one of these baton ideas.

● Play the game Follow the Tapper. Tap gently on something in the room, and let the child imitate you. Then have the child choose something to tap on and you follow his or her lead.

● Give directions that incorporate the batons, such as "Touch your nose," "Tap your toes," "Touch the floor," and "Turn around."

● Pretend to be the "traffic police" and play Stop and Go. Tell the child to walk around the room when your baton is held up but when it's down, to stop. Take turns being the police officer.

● Lay the batons on the floor and recite "Jack Be Nimble, Jack Be Quick." When "Jack jumps over the candlestick," hop over the batons.

Terry Tooth

Discovery

Developmental Skill:

The child will learn about TEETH.

Simple Supplies:

You'll need a small mirror, a marker, thin apple slices, a toothbrush, a crayon, and a white paper tooth. Use the Terry Tooth illustration in the margin as a pattern.

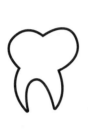

Set the apple slices, mirror, and toothbrush beside you. Hold up the paper tooth and ask: **What is this?** Tell the child it is a pretend tooth, and ask the child to point to his or her teeth. Then point to your teeth and say: **Here are my teeth. See? God made our teeth to help us eat good food. Teeth are shiny. Teeth are white. And teeth can chew—chomp! chomp! chomp! Can you chomp your teeth?** Pause for the child to respond. Then say: **Let's look at our teeth.**

Hold up the mirror, and let the child smile and look closely at his or her teeth. Point to your front and back teeth and say: **These are front teeth. They bite apples. And these are back teeth. They chew apples.** Hand the child a slice of apple to bite and chew. As the child nibbles the apple slice, hold up the toothbrush. Say: **Teeth need to be clean after they bite and chew. What is this?** Pause for response. **Toothbrushes clean teeth. Brush-a-brush-a-brush them clean.** Rub the toothbrush across the paper tooth, then let the child do the same. **Then teeth are happy!** Draw a happy face on the paper tooth.

Hold up the smiling tooth and say: **This is Terry Tooth. Let's play a fun game. I'll hide Terry Tooth, then you can find it. Close your eyes!** Place the paper tooth in plain sight. Then let the child find Terry Tooth. Play the game several more times, then let the child hide the tooth.

Play Pointer

Use discovery play to help teach beginning hygienic habits. Discovering hands leads to washing them, exploring hair leads to brushing it, looking at noses leads to tissues.

Partner Play

"**Jonathan** said to David, 'Go in peace.
We have promised by the Lord
that we will be friends.'"
1 SAMUEL 20:42A

Understanding the Stage

What's cuter than a young child with his or her first real playmate? They giggle, whisper, trade toys, and become consumed by the act of playing together. It's almost cause for tears when Jason or Jamie can't play! Partner play marks the stage of development where a child actually invites another child into his or her circle of entertainment. More willing to share, ready to hear and offer new ideas, and the heady autonomy that comes with having a "special friend all my own" are earmarks of partner play.

Babies and very young toddlers need initiated activities, but children ages three to five take charge of their own play. Often innovative, sometimes imitative, but always emancipated, these children demand freedom and fun in their playtimes—and their playmates. Whether they're staging a spaceship launch, exploring the properties of wet sand, or tossing beanbags, partner play is marked by self-initiation, an expanding social circle, and growing creativity. As the child grows, partner play will help the child learn how to develop long-lasting friendships—friendships characterized in the Bible by Ruth and Naomi, David and Jonathan, and Paul and Silas.

Partner play is the stage where emotional and social growth take giant leaps—a child begins to bemoan the fact that there's "no one to play with!" Happy for other children and stimulated by how peers think and react, children in the stage of partner play will only occasionally choose to play alone. With the advent of real playmates, the doors open wide to expose a world of more organized games and activities, cooperative relays, discovery centers, and simple games of skill.

The following games and activities all center around partner play and are designed to stimulate a child's sense of creativity, spatial concepts, conversation, and discovery. Each activity is based on one of the four play types discussed in this book's introduction. You'll also find a stated learning goal and valuable "Play Pointers" that offer tips and insights into your child's development.

> **Playing alone is a lonely "one"—**
> **But "two" will double all the fun!**
> **God brought a buddy to play with me.**
> **A dynamic duo—that's us—whee!**

The Games

Bowl Me Over

Spatial

Developmental Skill:

Your child will learn NUMBER NAMES.

Simple Supplies:

You'll need a small ball and six paper cups. Write the numeral one on two cups, the numeral two on two cups, and the numeral three on two cups.

Have children sit about five feet apart with their legs spread. Hand each child a set of number cups, and show children how to set up the paper cups with the numbers facing the other person. Have partners set up their cups.

Challenge children to roll the ball back and forth and aim for the paper cups that belong to

Play Pointer

Skill games are one of the best ways to increase a child's motor skill prowess. But be careful not to turn simple games of skill into competitions. Young children need to explore their physical capabilities without fear of failure.

their partners. When a cup is toppled, the person who rolled the ball calls out the number on the toppled cup. Continue until one partner has bowled over all his or her cups. Then set up the cups for another game.

Slightly older children will enjoy the challenge of bowling over the cups in sequential order. Or have children stack the cups bottom to bottom, and top to top, then bowl over the towers. Older children will also delight in rolling two small balls at once. Use foam balls or tennis balls.

When the game is over, encourage partners to give each other a high five and say, "Nice bowling, partner!" Have children help put the cups and balls away.

Picture Packs

Conversational

Developmental Skill:

Your child will learn about SHARING IDEAS.

Simple Supplies:

You'll need paper lunch sacks, scissors, glue, index cards or poster board, and magazines or old wallpaper books. Toy catalogs, animal magazines, and food magazines are perfect for this activity.

Cut out a variety of magazine pictures or wallpaper patterns and mount them on index cards or poster board. Place the picture cards in paper lunch sacks. Prepare one "picture pack" containing at least six pictures for each pair of children.

Help children get into pairs, and hand each pair a picture pack. Explain that they can look at the pictures together and tell why they like certain pictures or patterns. Then let each child choose a favorite picture to show everyone in the room. Have each pair stand and hold up its choices. Encourage partners to tell what pictures they've chosen, then have everyone clap. Continue until each pair has shared its pictures.

Use one or more of the following ideas to encourage children to interact with their partners.

● Have partners take turns laying down pictures in a row or domino-style. Then alternate turns pointing at pictures and having the partner tell the name of that illustration or the colors in the wallpaper pattern.

● Let a partner draw a card from the picture pack. Have the other child try to guess which picture it is.

Partner Books

Creative

Developmental Skill:
Your child will learn about IMAGINATION.

Simple Supplies:
You'll need a variety of pillows, colorful picture books, and cuddly stuffed animals. You can also provide a simple snack of crackers and juice.

Find a cozy corner of the room and scatter pillows and pictures books. Place the stuffed animals in the center of the room, and invite children to each choose a "cuddly partner" to enjoy books with.

Say: **God wants us to be kind to each other. That means we can share with our friends and help them when they need help. God likes it when we're kind to others. Let's practice kindness by being kind to these stuffed animals.** Then invite children to select a book and pillow. If you're short on pillows, use soft carpet squares or small blankets. Then simply let children enjoy the picture books with their make-believe partner friends. Encourage children to "read" the books to their partners by telling about the pictures. When a child has finished with a book, invite him or her to choose another.

Play Pointer

It's quite normal for young children to have imaginary friends—and they *do* serve a purpose. Child psychologists point out that imaginary friends may help ease separation anxiety, loneliness, and fear. Though imaginary friends can never take the place of warm hugs and cuddles, they *do* offer a measure of solace and security to young children.

End the book party by serving crackers and juice and letting children "share" their treats with the cuddly partners. Older children may enjoy giving their partners names, then introducing them to the class.

Moving Day

Spatial

Developmental Skill:
Your child will learn MOTOR SKILLS.

Simple Supplies:
You'll need medium-sized boxes or laundry baskets and a variety of toys and books.

Have children get with partners. Say: **Abram was a man in the Bible who moved. God told Abram to pack his things and move to a special land. Let's pretend that today is Abram's moving day. We can pack our toys and things in these boxes** (or baskets). **Then you and your partner can carry the box across the room and unpack it.** Let children pack their moving boxes and carry them to the opposite end of the room. Then have children cooperatively place the contents of the boxes on the floor and return for another load before reversing the moving process.

When everything has been moved and replaced, let children take turns "riding" in the make-believe moving vans. Let one partner sit in the box while the other partner pushes it a short way. Then have partners switch roles. If your group is slightly older, try a group activity. Have one child sit in the moving van while the class becomes the "engine" and cooperatively pushes the van. Be sure everyone has a turn being the truck driver.

The Chicken and the Egg

Conversational

Developmental Skill:
Your child will learn about TAKING TURNS.

Simple Supplies:
You'll need construction paper, a marker, glue, small paper wads, and an empty egg carton for each pair of children. If you can find stickers of chickens and roosters, your game will be even more fun.

Before this activity, cut out three paper egg-shapes and one circle from white construction paper. Draw a red comb, a beak, and eyes on the white circle to make a "rooster."

Cut two paper circles from yellow construction paper. Draw eyes and beaks on the yellow circles to make "chickens." Glue the eggs and circles at random in the empty egg cups.

Write a number in each of the remaining egg cups. Use numbers one, two, three, and four. You'll have to use some numbers more than once. Place a small paper wad inside each egg carton. Prepare a game carton for each pair of children.

Have children form pairs. Say: **I have a riddle for you. See if you know who I am.**

I have a pretty comb sitting on my head.
My feathers are white, but my comb is red.
I wake up early—I wake you, too—
With a cock-a-doodle-doodle-do!
Who am I?

Help children discover that the answer is a rooster. Then see if children can sound like chickens ("cluck-cluck"), and curl on the floor like eggs.

Tell children that you'll play a game called The Chicken and the Egg. Hand each pair an egg carton game. Explain that one partner closes the carton, turns it upside down and shakes it. Then he or she opens the carton to see where the paper wad landed.

Play Pointer

Children in the stage of partner play can begin learning simple game rules that involve taking turns. Keep game rules simple and few—and affirm children when they're doing a good job taking turns during play.

If the paper wad is on a number, his or her partner claps that many times; if it's on a chicken, the child says "cluck-cluck"; if it's on a rooster, the child crows; if it lands on an egg shape, the child curls up on the floor. Then the other partner takes a turn shaking the carton. Continue playing the game until each partner has had several chances to shake the game carton.

Store the game cartons in a convenient place for quick and easy use. If your children are slightly older, help them make their own "chicken and egg" games to take home and play.

Steppingstones

Spatial

Developmental Skill:
Your child will learn large MOTOR SKILLS.

Simple Supplies:
You'll need construction paper and masking tape. You may also wish to provide lively praise music.

You'll need one sheet of construction paper for every pair of children. Tape sheets of construction paper to the floor in a circle with each "steppingstone" about two feet apart. Make sure all the edges of the construction paper are firmly taped to the floor.

Help children find partners, and have each pair stand on a steppingstone together. Be sure all children are facing the same direction. Say: **We can play a fun game called Steppingstones. When I say "go," you and your partner can hop to the next steppingstone. Keep hopping until you've gone all the way around the circle.** Begin the game, and add lively "hopping" music if you wish.

When children have hopped around the circle, have them turn and go the opposite way. Then say: **Now let's pretend we're little frogs on lily pads. When I say, "Hop, little frogs," you and your partner hop to a different lily pad.** Play this variation several times. If your children are older, have them find new partners halfway through the game.

When you're finished playing, have children give a group clap to show how much fun it is to play with partners.

Partner Pizzas

Spatial

Developmental Skill:
Your child will learn about SHAPES.

You'll need scissors and large envelopes or pizza boxes. You'll also need felt in the following colors: brown, tan, red, yellow, and green.

Before this activity, you'll need to make one or two felt pizzas. For each felt pizza, cut an eight-inch circle of tan "crust" and a slightly smaller circle of red "sauce." Cut out several large yellow triangles and stars of "cheese," several orange rectangles and ovals of "meat," and a few green hearts and circles of "green pepper." Store the felt pizza pieces in a large envelope or a real pizza box.

Let partners play with the felt pizzas and take turns adding "ingredients" and identifying the different shapes and colors. As partners play, tell them that God is happy when we work together and share. If partners are a bit older, they might like to count the pieces they add to their pizzas. Use some of the following ideas with your perky pizza play.

Play Pointer

Young children greatly enjoy playing with felt shapes and pieces. They're inexpensive, colorful, and can be used again and again in a myriad of ways. The only limit? A child's imagination!

● Make individual snack pizzas. Use refrigerator biscuits for dough, pizza sauce, and grated cheese. Bake in a toaster oven at 350 degrees for fifteen minutes or until the dough is golden brown and the cheese is melted.

● Challenge your children to tell the sequence of the items when making a pizza. For example, first comes the crust, then the sauce, then the cheese, and so on.

● Pick up cardboard pizza rounds at a pizza parlor. Then let children tear "ingredients" from colored construction paper and glue them to the cardboard with glue sticks to make pretend pizzas.

Rainbows

Discovery

Developmental Skill:

Your child will learn about COLORS.

Simple Supplies:

You'll need colored tissue paper, plain paper, tape, newspaper, cotton swabs, liquid starch, small bowls, and scissors.

Cover a table with newspaper, and pour liquid starch into small bowls. Tape two sheets of paper together, short end to short end, for each pair of children. Tear tissue paper into small shapes and pieces and place them in piles on the table.

Hold up pieces of tissue paper, and ask children to identify the colors. Say: **Do you know who made the first rainbow? God made the rainbow. God made the beautiful rainbow to show us his love. All the colors put together make a beautiful rainbow. We can make pretty rainbows together. Put some starch on your papers, then add a piece of tissue paper. You can even put two pieces of tissue paper together to make a new color!** Demonstrate how to spread liquid starch on the paper using a cotton swab. Then tear a piece of tissue paper and stick it on the wet starch. Then have children find partners and hand each pair a double sheet of paper. Say: **See how many colors you and your partner can add to your beautiful rainbow.**

Circulate and make comments such as "You and your partner are making such a nice picture" and "I like the way you're taking turns with the starch and tissue paper." Remind children that God makes real rainbows, but pretend rainbows are pretty too.

> ### Play Pointer
> Cooperative crafts are fun for children and a valuable way for them to share ideas and personal tastes.

When the pictures are finished, write the partners' names on the front. Encourage children to work in pairs to help you clean up the area. When the pictures are dry, invite partners to each hold a side of their pictures and show the class their beautiful rainbows. Display the pictures on a wall or door for everyone to enjoy. Cut the pictures in half when you're ready to send them home.

Hop Like a Froggy

Creative

Developmental Skill:
Your child will learn large MOTOR SKILLS.

Simple Supplies:
none

Say: **God made all the animals in the world. Animals are different from people. Some are smaller and some are larger. And many animals move about in different ways than people do. Let's pretend that we're some of God's marvelous animals.**

Have children find partners to act out these fun animal motions. Encourage partners to stay close together and make animal noises. Repeat the following rhyme. Then invite each pair of children to choose what animal they'd like to repeat a second time.

Hop like a froggy,
Have a little fun.
Hop, hop, hop—
Now the froggy's done.

Creep like a lizard,
Have a little fun.
Creep, creep, creep—
Now the lizard's done.

Swim like a fishy,
Have a little fun.
Swish, swash, swishy—
Now the fishy's done.

Here's some more animals the partners can imitate.

● Stomp like an elephant...
● Fly like a butterfly...
● Waddle like a duck...
● Prance like a pony...

When you're done, you may wish to serve animal crackers and juice as a special treat. Let partners each hand the other an animal shape and say, "Thanks for being a fun partner."

Love Those Leaves

Discovery

Developmental Skill:
Your child will learn about NATURE.

Simple Supplies:
You'll need paper lunch sacks, paper, clothes hangers, string, and tape.

This activity is best suited for a sunny autumn day. Have children find partners, and hand each pair a lunch sack. Write children's names on their sacks. Lead children outside on a "leaf safari," and have partners collect the leaves they think are prettiest. Encourage partners to take turns holding the paper sack—one child holds the sack, while the other picks up leaves.

When the leaf hunt is over, go inside and invite partners to examine their natural treasures. Tell children that the Bible tells us God created all the trees. Point out how God made the bumpy veins to carry water and food to the leaves, and how God made leaves to come in many sizes, shapes, and colors. Challenge children to sort the leaves by color, size, or shape.

Play Pointer

Nature walks are great ways for young children to interact with partners. Use pairs of plastic pop-can rings that are still attached as "pal-holders." Have each partner hold a ring on the walk to keep children happily safe and together.

Then hand each child a clothes hanger and several pieces of string. Have children tape the leaves to the ends of the string, then tape the other ends to the clothes hangers to make mobiles. Encourage partners to help each other tape their leaves to the strings and clothes hangers. Write the children's names on the leaves, then hang the leafy mobiles in the room or hallway for everyone to enjoy.

For a fun variation, try one of these ideas.

● Collect leaves, then show children how to brush paint over one side of a leaf, then "stamp" the leaf onto the paper.

● Trace around real leaves, and cut the shapes from poster board. Then have an adult helper trace the patterns on fabric squares using permanent ink. Let partners use nontoxic fabric paint or washable markers to decorate pretty "doilies" to give as gifts.

● If you have older children, have partners help each other place sheets of paper over real leaves, then gently color over the leaves. The leaf outlines and veins will "magically" appear on the paper!

Potato Patch

Conversational

Developmental Skill:
Your child will learn about COOPERATION.

Simple Supplies:
You'll need a sandbox with sand, spoons, and small raw potatoes.

If you don't have a sandbox, make one by filling a dishpan with sand available at most hardware, lumber, and building stores.

Place the spoons and potatoes beside the sandbox. Explain to the partners that one is the Potato Planter and the other is the Potato Picker. The Potato Planter uses a spoon to "plant" potatoes while the partner hides his or her eyes. Then the Potato Picker uses a spoon to "dig up" the potatoes. Have children switch roles often. Encourage partners to pretend they're potato farmers and talk about planting or picking potatoes, count the number of potatoes, and tell what potatoes need to grow.

This is a fun activity to use with any raw vegetables. Have children "plant" carrots, radishes, beans, and small onions. Or they can even have a smaller "garden" and plant peanuts in the shell!

For extra fun, let children wash the raw vegetables, then have an adult helper peel and cut them up to make yummy vegetable soup. Use the Vegetable Soup recipe, and serve the soup in paper cups or bowls.

Vegetable Soup

Place 6 cups water, a 15-ounce can tomato sauce, ½ teaspoon salt, and 2 to 3 cups raw vegetables in a pot. Be sure the vegetables are cut into bite-sized pieces. Cook and simmer until the vegetables are tender—about 30 minutes. Then stir in a small package of alphabet noodles. Cook until the noodles are done—about 10 minutes. Season to taste with seasoned salt, pepper, and dried parsley.

Match Me!

Spatial

Developmental Skill:
Your child will learn about NUMBERS.

Simple Supplies:
You'll need colorful markers, index cards, and a large envelope.

Before this partner activity, prepare number cards by drawing sheep on one side of the index cards. Refer to the drawing below for guidance. Use one, two, three, four, or five sheep. Then on the reverse sides, draw colorful geometric shapes including a star, heart, circle, triangle, and square. Make another set just like this one. You'll need two sets of identical cards for each pair of children.

Have children find partners, and hand each child a set of cards. Tell children to put the cards on the floor so they see only sheep or only geometric shapes. Then show how one partner holds up a card and his or her partner holds up the matching card. Have partners take turns going first. Encourage partners to tell each other the number of sheep, the color, or the shape as cards are held up.

Older children may enjoy a special challenge. Draw sheep on one side of each card and a corresponding numeral on the reverse side. Then have one partner place the cards "sheep up" and the other partner place his or her cards "numerals up." When sheep are pointed to, the other partner must point to the corresponding numeral and vice versa.

Keep the "match me" cards in a large envelope for easy retrieval. You may wish to cover the cards with clear self-adhesive paper to make them more durable.

Tiger Tail

Creative

Developmental Skill:

Your child will learn about IMAGINATION.

Simple Supplies:

You'll need newspaper, orange crepe paper, scissors, and washable black markers.

Cut the crepe paper into a two-foot "tail" for each child. Cover a table with newspaper, and set out the markers. Have children get into pairs, then hand each child a paper tail. Have partners share markers and color black stripes on the orange tails.

Then tell children to tuck the tails into their waistbands, or you can tape the tails to their clothing. Explain that these are pretend tiger tails. Say: **Let's play a partner game with our tiger tails. I'll say a rhyme and you can follow what the words say.** Repeat the following rhyme and have children act out the actions with their partners.

Tap your partner on the toes—
Swing your tiger tail!
Touch your partner on the nose—

Swing your tiger tail!
Shake your partner's little hand—
Swing your tiger tail!
Now growl "hello" and "I like you!"
Swing your tiger tail!

Have children change partners and repeat the rhyme game. Let children wear their tiger tails as you pretend to walk like tigers, eat like tigers, run like tigers, growl like tigers, and sleep like tigers! For a fun way to end playtime, serve animal crackers and listen to a Winnie-the-Pooh story starring Tigger.

Snowball Catch

Spatial

Developmental Skill:
Your child will learn large MOTOR SKILLS.

Simple Supplies:
You'll need pairs of white socks. You may also wish to have wintry-type music such as "Jingle Bells" or "Winter Wonderland" playing in the background.

R oll the socks into balls, and hand each pair of children a "snowball." Have children stand facing each other about three feet apart. Say: **What's cold and white and falls from the sky? Snow! And God made snow to cover the ground to look pretty and play with! It's not snowing outside, but we can pretend to have some shivery fun inside. Let's toss snowballs gently back and forth to our partners.** Demonstrate how to toss a snowball—not throw it. Have children toss the snowballs back and forth.

You may wish to play a "wintry" cassette or sing the words to "Jingle Bells" without musical accompaniment.

After a few minutes, say: **Now sit down and see if you can toss snowballs back and forth.** After children have tossed snowballs sitting down, have them kneel and toss snowballs and then roll them back and forth.

Try a few of these snappy snowball variations.

● Have partners each place a book at their feet and try to toss the snowball onto the books.

● See if partners can gently roll the snowballs across the room by

> ### Play Pointer
> Large motor skills include hopping, skipping, running, tiptoeing, and tossing balls. Bouncy playground balls, tennis balls, and foam rubber balls are all safe, but may be better suited for outdoor games. Socks on the other hand make super soft play balls for inside games and activities.

pushing them back and forth with their feet.

● Let partners invent "I can do that" tricks. Have one partner do a snowball trick, such as balancing the snowball on his or her head. Then see if the other partner can do the same trick.

Oceans of Fun

Discovery

Developmental Skill:
Your child will learn about MOTION.

Simple Supplies:
You'll need a large towel and a stuffed animal for each pair of children. You may also bring fish-shaped crackers for a simple snack.

Say: **God made the oceans, and God made fish. Let's have fun playing a game about the ocean.**

Hand partners a large towel and a small stuffed animal. Demonstrate how to hold the towel on each end and place the stuffed animal in the center. Show children how to make "ripples and waves" by gently shaking and moving the towel back and forth. Point out how the moving towel causes the stuffed animal to move.

Ask children if they think the stuffed animal is having fun going for a pretend swim. Let children experiment with how big they can make the waves without letting the stuffed animal fall to the floor. Challenge children to make waves with the towel held on the floor, then high in the air. You may wish to let children add one or two more stuffed animals for a real "pool party"!

Lead partners in repeating the following rhyme as they make the stuffed animal swim.

Glub, glub, glub-
I'm a great big fish.
Glub, glub, glub—
Watch me swim and swish!

End playtime by inviting partners to sit on their towels and nibble fish-shaped crackers.

Dough Duos

Discovery

Your child will learn about COLORS.

You'll need modeling dough in a variety of colors and an airtight plastic bag.

Either purchase ready-made modeling dough or use the recipe here to make your own. You'll need at least two colors of modeling dough.

No-Cook Modeling Dough

Mix 1 cup cold water, 1 cup salt, 2 teaspoons vegetable oil. Stir in 3 cups flour and 2 tablespoons cornstarch. Knead on a cutting board until the dough is soft and pliable. Divide the dough and knead different shades of food coloring into each lump of dough. Using paste food coloring will make brightly colored dough. Store the dough in an airtight bag. Note: This dough is soft and bright, but doesn't air-dry well.

Hand each pair two lumps of different-colored dough—red and yellow dough, for example. Encourage partners to tell each other the colors they're holding and then make things that are those colors. For example, a red apple or a yellow star. See if partners can identify what each other has made.

Then have children each pinch off three pieces of dough. Tell them each to hand one piece to their partners and to set another piece aside. Then invite each child to mix the last piece of dough with the dough from his or her partner to make a new color. See if pairs can identify the new colors made and make something that is that color. For example, red and yellow dough would make orange, and a child could make an orange pumpkin from the dough.

Play Pointer

In this exciting activity, young children gladly share bits of dough to make new colors—but don't expect easy sharing all the time! Look for games and activities that encourage sharing, then nurture children with affirming comments about how nicely they share and cooperate.

Encourage children to trade bits of dough and make more new colors. Ask children to identify the new colors. You may wish to put each child's dough in a plastic sandwich bag to send home. Consider copying the recipe and stapling it to the bag for make-at-home fun.

Hanging Out Together

Conversational

Developmental Skill:
Your child will learn about PAIRS.

Simple Supplies:
You'll need a clothesline, hinge-style clothespins, and pairs of socks, mittens, and gloves.

If you need more pairs of items than you can hunt up, cut simple sock and mitten shapes from matching patterns of gift wrap or wallpaper. String the clothesline across one end of the room, and clip clothespins to the clothesline. Have children find partners to "hang up the wash." Demonstrate how to pinch the clothespins together to open them, and how to attach socks, mittens, and gloves to the clothesline. Caution children about getting fingers caught in the clothespins. Then invite partners to help each other hang up a pile of "wash."

As children are playing, say: **Do you see how there are two socks and two mittens and two gloves? Two of the same things are called a "pair." We wear a pair of socks and a pair of shoes. We buy a pair of mittens. We put on a pair of gloves. Pairs go together. Did you know that partners are pairs? You and your partner are a pair of friends! And pairs of friends help each other, just as you're doing. Now can you take down the pairs of socks, mittens, and gloves? Then you can hang them up again.**

Let children take turns hanging the wash and taking it down. Challenge older children to think of other things that come in pairs, such as boots and earmuffs.

As children play, remind them of how happy God is when we help each other. Challenge children to help at home by sorting the wash or hanging up wash to dry.

Bedtime Puppies

Conversational

Developmental Skill:
Your child will learn about COUNTING.

Simple Supplies:
You'll need nine-by-twelve-inch envelopes, a marker, and small black felt

circles. You'll also need photocopies of the "Bedtime Puppies" handout from page 54.

Glue the "Bedtime Puppies" page to the front of a large envelope. Color the picture if you wish. Place thirteen small black felt circles inside the envelope. Prepare one game envelope for each pair of children.

Have children form pairs, and hand each pair a "Bedtime Puppies" game envelope. Say: **What do you see in the picture? Lots of puppies! Sleepy puppies in snuggly beds. But the puppies don't have any spots. We can help the puppies find their spots. Look at the number of dots on each puppy's bed. Now put that many felt "spots" on the puppy. See if you can help all the sleepy puppies find their spots.**

Have children place the felt circles in piles beside the game envelopes. Then tell them to take turns counting out felt circles and placing them on the puppies. When all the felt circles have been used up, have the partners say, "Good night, puppies."

This simple-to-prepare game makes a fun take-home craft project, too. Let children color photocopies of the "Bedtime Puppies" page, then glue the copies to the front of large envelopes. Hand each child thirteen felt circles to place inside the game envelope. Encourage children to show their families how to play this game at bedtime! Then offer a bedtime prayer thanking God for sweet sleep and the nice day just passed.

Play Pointer

Simple board games are perfect for children in partner play. They learn about taking turns and following directions while having loads of fun. Keep the rules simple, the game board colorful, and the fun will flow!

Bedtime Puppies

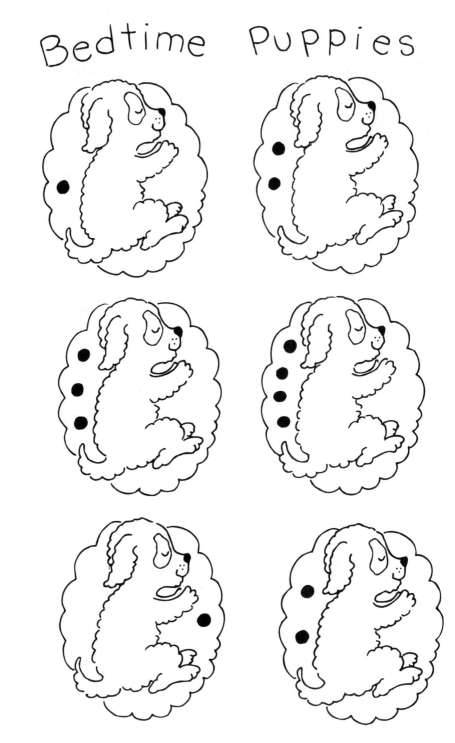

Burger Shop

Creative

Developmental Skill

Your child will learn SEQUENTIAL ORDER.

Simple Supplies:

You'll need markers, colored construction paper, and scissors. You'll also need foam or cardboard burger boxes available at most fast-food chains.

Before this activity, prepare paper burgers: Cut two five-inch circles of light brown construction paper for the bun (or color white construction paper with light brown crayon). Draw sesame seeds on one circle for the top bun.

Cut a four-inch circle of dark brown paper for meat, and two smaller red construction paper circles for tomato slices. Use markers to add "seeds" to the tomatoes. Cut two four-inch squares of orange or yellow construction paper for "cheese." Tear out several green "lettuce leaves" and "pickles."

Put the paper hamburger together in the following order: bottom bun, meat, lettuce, cheese, tomatoes, pickles, and top bun. Place the burger in a burger box. Prepare one burger box for each pair of children.

> ### Play Pointer
>
> Games and activities with realistic-looking components are a draw to young children's imaginations. As children play with their burger boxes, encourage them to pretend they're ordering real burgers or working at a hamburger stand. Conversation and imagination will grow—and so will the fun!

Hand each pair of children a burger box. Let children take turns constructing paper burgers and challenge them to remember the order the items were placed—cheese then tomatoes or lettuce then cheese, for example. Older children can take turns making burgers for their partners, then have partners make burgers for them. If you want to try a group activity, let children make their burgers at the same time as children take turns calling out the order of food items.

Roads 'n' Rides

Creative

Developmental Skill:

Your child will learn about COOPERATION.

You'll need a solid-color bedsheet, clear packing tape, washable markers, and small toy cars.

This partner play activity is super rainy day fun—and keeps young children happy and engaged for hours.

Spread an old sheet face down on the floor. Tape the edges to the floor to prevent slippage. Let children use washable markers to draw roads, houses, trees, stop signs, and buildings.

Encourage children to work together to make a whole town. Then let children "drive" the cars along the roads and tour the town. Ask children to tell you about the town and the buildings. When they're finished playing, store the foldaway town for the next rainy day. Children will be excited to play with their special creation again and again.

For fun variations, use one or more of the following building ideas.

● Provide building blocks, small boxes, and paper cups to use as buildings, tunnels, and bridges.

● Use the play mat to stimulate talk about neighborhoods, communities and community helpers, and how roads help people.

● Turn the play mat into a beanbag game. Let children toss beanbags or peanuts onto the mat and tell what pictures the bags land on, such as streets, houses, or stop signs.

Silly Stories

Conversational

Developmental Skill:

Your child will learn about STORY WORDS.

Simple Supplies:

You'll need index cards, tape, scissors, and old magazines.

Cut out magazine pictures of food, toys, cars, animals, people, and furniture. Tape or glue the pictures to index cards.

Hand partners six or more picture cards. Encourage children to tell each other about the pictures. Then say: **We like stories. And we learn from stories. Jesus told a lot of stories to teach people about love, being kind, and about God. Some stories are fun, some are sad, some are exciting, and some stories are silly. You can help me tell a silly story. I'll read the words, and when I point to you, hold up a card and tell** what the picture is. We'll take turns holding up cards so everyone will have a chance to help tell the silly story.

Play Pointer

Children love simple, silly stories—especially when they take an active role in storytelling. Picture cards are an invaluable aid that encourage children to verbalize words and create their own stories.

Read the following story, and let partners take turns holding up cards at the appropriate places in the story. Encourage children to tell the picture names as they hold the cards up.

Once there was a big (picture). **It lived in a pretty** (picture). **The** (repeat picture name) **was very hungry—but what could it eat? Could it eat a** (picture)? **Or a** (picture)? **Or would it rather eat a** (picture)? **The** (repeat picture name) **decided to eat a** (picture) **for breakfast. And yum-yum-yummy, it was good!** Have children rub their tummies.

Repeat the story a few more times. Each time you retell the story, it will be fresh and funny as the pictures change. After a few repetitions, most children will be able to repeat the story without your help!

Fruit Matchups

Spatial

Developmental Skill:
Your child will learn COLORS AND MATCHING SKILLS.

Simple Supplies:
You'll need colored construction paper, envelopes, and scissors. You may also provide a simple snack of fruit pieces.

Before this activity, cut pairs of fruit from colored construction paper. Use the illustrations on page 58 as patterns. Cut out red apples, yellow bananas, orange oranges, blue blueberries, green limes, and two bunches of purple grapes. Place the fruit pairs in envelopes, putting several different fruit pairs in each envelope—two apples, two oranges, and two bananas, for example. You'll need one envelope for every two children.

Say: **God gives us good food to eat. God made fruit for us to eat—it tastes good and helps us stay healthy. Let's play a game with fruit.**

Help children find partners, and give each pair an envelope. Challenge children to work together to match fruits by type and color and then tell the name of each fruit and its color. Then have each partner hide one of each fruit in his or her lap. When you count to three, have partners each pick a fruit and place it on the floor. If a match is made, partners can give each other a high five. If a match isn't made, have children hide the fruits again for the next round. Continue playing for several rounds.

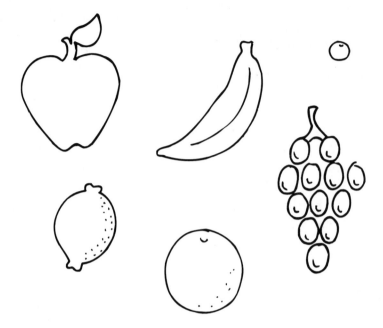

End your fruity game by serving fruit pieces to nibble.

Here are several variations of the Fruit Matchups game to try.

● Let older children think up funny fruit names by putting two different fruits together. For example, they might make an "applenana" (apple and banana) or a "grapel" (grape and apple).

● Hide the fruits around the room, and let partners search for the "yummies." Have each child find one of each fruit.

● Set out real apples, bananas, grapes, limes, oranges, and blueberries. Have children match the paper fruits to the real ones, then cut open the real ones for a fruity tasting party. Encourage children to taste each fruit and tell what it's like. They can compare and contrast which fruits are sweet, sour, smooth, crunchy, and juicy.

Twin Turtles

Creative

Developmental Skill:

Your child will learn about IMAGINATION.

Simple Supplies:

You'll need a bath or beach towel for each pair of children.

Have children get with partners. Hand each pair of children a large towel or "turtle shell." Say: **I have a riddle for you. See if you can guess what animal I am.**

I'm small and cute and pretty green—
I'm very, very s-l-o-w.
I carry my house upon my back
Everywhere I go.
What am I?

Have children guess that the answer is a turtle. Then say: **Let's pretend we're twin turtles. Get on your hands and knees beside your partner. I'll put pretend turtle shells on your backs. Then we'll say a rhyme while you crawl like turtles. Stay beside your partner. Remember, you're twin turtles!**

Place a towel on the backs of each pair of children. Then repeat the following action rhyme several times, helping children with the actions.

Little turtles, little turtles *(crawl slowly)*,
Crawl so slow.
Little turtles, little turtles *(crawl slowly)*,
On you go.

Little turtles, little turtles *(crawl slowly)*,
Hide inside—yoo-hoo. *(Pull heads under the towel "shell.")*
Little turtles, little turtles *(stay hidden)*,
Peekaboo! *(Poke heads out of shell.)*

Balancing Game

Discovery

Developmental Skill:
Your child will learn the concept of BALANCING.

Simple Supplies:
You'll need fishing line, rulers, tape, and paper plates. You'll also need small treats, such as marshmallows, chocolate chips, and cereal.

Before this activity, make "scales" by taping a three-foot length of fishing line to the center of a ruler. Be sure the ruler is balanced as it hangs from the fishing line. Tape a paper plate on each end of the ruler and again make sure the ruler balances when suspended. Tape the other end of the fishing line from a table so the ruler hangs in balance. Place the treats under the scale.

Let partners experiment with placing treats on each paper plate and seeing if they can keep the scale from tipping too much and spilling the treats. Encourage partners to place one morsel at a time on the paper plates and watch how the ends of the scale tip or balance. Explain that balancing the scale means the scale is even and not tipped.

Next, have children take turns eating one morsel at a time from the paper plates to see if they can keep the scales balanced until all the treats are gone.

Play Pointer
Young children love experimenting with scales. Consider purchasing a small, inexpensive food scale and letting children "weigh out" items to see which are heavier.

Older children may enjoy "weighing" items. Using cereal loops, chocolate chips, feathers, or a mixture of many items, let children predict which items are heavier than others. Or they can experiment balancing items on the scale—does it take three chocolate chips to balance one small marshmallow?

Row Your Boat

Conversational

Developmental Skill:
Your child will learn COOPERATION.

Simple Supplies:
You'll need scissors and plastic pop-can holder rings. These are the rings that hold six-packs of soda pop together. You'll need two rings for each set of partners.

Cut the plastic pop holders into three sections to make pairs of two connected rings.

Have partners sit on the floor facing each other with their legs crossed. Say: **Sometimes Jesus traveled on boats. Jesus and his friends liked to sail in boats and even fished from their boats. Let's pretend that we're sitting in pretend boats with our partners. Can you feel the water rocking you back and forth?** Sway back and forth. **Back and forth, back and forth—it's a nice day for sailing in a row boat. But we need oars to row our boats. Let's pretend that these holder rings are oars.** Hand an "oar" to each set of partners. **Each of you can hold a ring with both hands, and we'll sing a song as we row our boats.**

Lead children in singing "Row, Row, Row Your Boat" as they move back and forth in "rowing" motions while holding the plastic rings. Sing the song a couple of times.

Row, row, row your boat
Gently down the stream.
Merrily, merrily, merrily, merrily—
Life is but a dream.

After children have "rowed the boat" a few times, have partners stand and pretend they're driving buses using the plastic rings as steering wheels. Invite them to "motor" around the room while singing another verse.

Drive, drive, drive the bus
All around the town.
Merrily, merrily, merrily, merrily—
Drive it all around.

Use the additional verses below or invite children to make up their own words.

- Drive the tractor…all around the farm
- Pull the wagon…all around the town
- Fly the airplane…all around the sky

Peer Play

" 'I call you friends.' "
JOHN 15:15B

Understanding the Stage

They've arrived! Full-fledged playmates—in plural! Peer play marks the stage where children are ready to accept a wide range of friends and playmates. A child's circle of entertainment is now large enough to accommodate small groups and even entire classes—and invitations are freely extended to "c'mon in and play!"

You can think of peer play as "group play"—where a child freely interacts with peers on all levels: emotionally, intellectually, physically, conceptually, and conversationally. The free exchange of thoughts and ideas and the acceptance of a wide range of peers makes peer play perhaps the most exciting stage of developmental play in all childhood. But the stage is not without bumps.

Peer play is at once the easiest and most difficult stage of play. It seems a natural move from the twosome of partner play to the three-and-more-some of peer play. But with more friends come more problems in communication, acceptance, and self-esteem. If a playmate doesn't like another child's choice of play, the playmate may feel inferior or sullen, or become withdrawn and decide to play alone. But not to worry! It's all just "child's play," and children *do* learn to cope and grow through the ups and downs of playtime.

Since the stage of peer play closely relates to the advent of school, letter and number games find an increasingly important role in playtime. Children begin to imitate teachers and play "school." They enjoy the independence of "I-can-do-it" workbooks and color-by-numbers pictures. Spatial concepts such as colors, sizes, weights, and shapes figure into children's games and are evidenced by their desire to build arch-and-span-type bridges, intricate block designs, and colorful towers that stretch the limits of imagination—and physics! No other stage of play melds so completely with what a child is learning about himself or herself and school. And no other stage can be such a fruitful time for children to learn that God brings us good friends to love and care for!

What are the best games and activities for peer play? Noncompetitive group games, races, relays, letter and number games, simple songs, and role-playing activities are winners for this stage of play. The following games and activities all focus on peer play and are designed to stimulate your child's sense of creativity, spatial concepts, conversation, and discovery—all within the realm of his or her relationship to peers. Each activity is based on one of the four play types discussed in the book's introduction.

I have so many pretty games
That bring me smiles of joy.
But though I have a million games,
Friends are my favorite "toy"!

The Games

Guard the Gorilla

Conversational

Developmental Skill:
Your child will learn large MOTOR SKILLS.

Simple Supplies:
You'll need six plastic tumblers, masking tape, and a playground ball.

This simple game is active and is best suited for a large, clear playing space. Place a masking tape line down the center of the playing area.

Have children line up the plastic tumbler "gorillas," about ten feet behind the masking tape line. Then have children line up between the tumblers and the tape line.

Play Pointer

Even young children have loads of fun with group games if you follow the three S's. Keep the games: simple, short, and shared (cooperative).

Say: **Pretend you're deep in the jungle. The tape line is a river you can't cross, and the plastic cups are gorillas you need to guard. I'll roll a ball across the river. You must all work together to guard the gorillas from being knocked down. Guard the gorillas by blocking the ball with your feet—but don't use your hands in this game! Ready? Let's get rolling!**

Roll the ball into the playing area, and let children kick it back to you.

When the gorillas are all knocked over, stop play and set them back up. Then continue the game. Let children play for several minutes. Then have children cheer. Say: **Good job! You all worked together to guard the gorillas.**

You may wish to end playtime by serving frozen treats called Monkey Tails. Cut peeled bananas in half, and poke a clean craft stick in one end of each banana half. Dip the bananas in melted chocolate, then freeze on wax paper.

Cooperative Banner

Creative

Developmental Skill:
Your child will learn TEAMWORK.

Simple Supplies:
You'll need shallow pans of tempera paint, a marker, newspaper, paintbrushes, and a roll of white shelf paper. Providing paint shirts for the children is a good idea. Also bring in old gym shoes with interesting treads and a variety of toy cars and trucks with wheels that turn.

Place newspaper on a flat surface, such as a large table, hard floor, or sidewalk. Roll out a five- or six-foot length of white shelf paper. Write the following words across the top: "Teamwork Gets Things Rolling!" Pour colored tempera paint into shallow pans and place them at different locations on the paper. Set the cars, trucks, and old gym shoes near the paper.

Gather children around the banner. Say: **Groups of friends can get a lot done when they work together. God likes it when we help one another and work together. When friends work together, it's called "teamwork." And today we'll have fun making a teamwork banner to hang. The words at the top of the banner say, "Teamwork Gets Things**

Rolling!" I'll show you how we can get rolling on our project.

Show children how to lightly dip the toy car and truck wheels in paint, then roll them across the banner. Demonstrate how to brush paint on the sole of a gym shoe and slip hands or feet inside to make footprints across the paper. Then let children freely create a colorful, cooperative banner. Remind them to be careful with the paint. Circulate and make affirming comments, such as "I like the way you're all working together," "God is pleased when we work together," and "Good friends make good teamwork."

When the banner is dry, help children sign their names to the banner. Then hang the banner on a wall, door, or in a hallway to show others your team pride. Tell children that banners help decorate churches to show others the love and joy they feel when worshiping God.

Small, Medium, Large

Discovery

Developmental Skill:
Your child will learn about SIZES.

Simple Supplies:
You'll need colored vinyl tape or masking tape and three balls—a small one, a medium one, and a large one.

Before this activity, make three tape circles on the floor. Make one circle one foot in diameter, one circle two feet in diameter, and one circle five feet in diameter. Be sure you have a small, medium, and large ball. Consider using a table tennis ball, a tennis ball, and a playground ball.

Gather children outside the circles at one end of the room. Place the three balls on the floor, but not in order of their sizes. Ask: **Who would like to find the small ball and place it here?** Have a child place the small ball off to one side. Then ask for someone to find the biggest ball and place it a foot away from the small ball. Finally, ask a volunteer to find the medium-sized ball and place it between the small and biggest ball.

Then point to the balls as you say: **These three balls are all different sizes. There's a small ball, a medium ball, and a large ball. Let's make small, medium, and large arm circles.** Lead the group in making arm circles from smallest to largest and from largest to smallest. Use the words small, medium, and large to describe the circles.

Then say: **We can play a game called Small, Medium, and Large. When I say "small," hop to the small circle and put your finger in it because your finger is small. When I say "medium," hop to the medium circle and put your hand in it** because your hand is medium-sized. **And when I say "large," hop to the large circle and put one foot in it because your foot is large. Ready? Small!** Let children hop to the circle and put their fingers on the floor inside the circle. Then call another size. Mix up the order you call the sizes and play several rounds.

Then let children take turns calling out sizes and vary the way children move between circles, such as crawling, walking backward, or tiptoeing.

Have children stand around the circles and bounce balls that correspond to the size of each circle. For example, let children around the medium-sized circle bounce a tennis ball to each other, making the ball bounce in the circle. After a few bounces, have children switch circles. Play until all children have visited each circle.

Kangaroo Romp

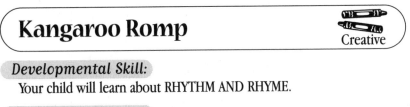

Creative

Developmental Skill:

Your child will learn about RHYTHM AND RHYME.

Simple Supplies:

Gather children in a circle and say: **I have a riddle for you. See if you can guess what animal I am.**

I like to hop and hop and hop. *(Hop three times.)*
You'll see me in the zoo. *(Hold hands to eyes like binoculars.)*
I keep my babies in my pouch. *(Pretend to put a baby in a pouch.)*
I am a (fill in the blank)! *(Cup your ear with your hand.)*

Help children discover that the answer is a kangaroo. Then say: **Kangaroos are one of God's most unusual animals. Just imagine what it would be like to hop all the time.** Hop and say: **Hoppity! Hoppity! Hoppity! Let's pretend we're a big family of kangaroos going for a** walk. I'll say the words, and you can follow my actions.

Lead children in the following action rhyme. Repeat the rhyme several times, and children will soon learn the words and rhythm.

Hop, hop *(hop on each word—hold arms upon your chest with hands bent outward)*,
Kangaroos. *(Wave your hands in the air.)*
Bippity-bop. *(Hop three times.)*
Let's get in rows of twos. *(Line up children in pairs.)*

Hop! Hop! *(Hop twice.)*
Hoppity-hop! *(Hop three times.)*
Hop! Hop! *(Hop twice.)*
Hoppity-hop! *(Hop three times.)*

Hop, hop *(hop on each word—hold arms upon your chest with hands bent outward)*,
Kangaroos. *(Wave your hands in the air.)*
Bippity-bop. *(Hop three times.)*
Let's put on kanga-shoes. *(Pretend to put on long kangaroo shoes.)*

Hop! Hop! *(Hop twice.)*
Hoppity-hop! *(Hop three times.)*
Hop! Hop! *(Hop twice.)*
Hoppity-hop! *(Hop three times.)*

Hop, hop *(hop on each word—hold arms upon your chest with hands bent outward)*,
Kangaroos. *(Wave your hands in the air.)*
Bippity-bop. *(Hop three times.)*
Let's take a little snooze! *(Fold hands under your head.)*

Letter Snatch

Conversational

Developmental Skill:
Your child will learn LETTER RECOGNITION.

Simple Supplies:
You'll need markers, index cards, and a large envelope.

Before this activity, decide which letters to work on, but limit the number to no more than six. Then prepare sets of letter cards by writing one letter on each index card. Make a set for every child and make one for yourself, too.

Scatter letter cards at one end of the room. Hold on to your set of letter cards. Gather children, and flash your letter cards one by one. Let children identify the letters several times. Then say: **There are letter cards for each of you at the other end of the room. I'll flash a letter card, then you hop to the other end of the room and find a card with the same letter. Bring the card and hop back here.**

Hold up a letter card to start the game. When all the children have returned with letter cards, have them hold the cards up high and call out the letter name. Then have them set the cards down, and hold up another letter. Continue until all the letter cards have been retrieved. Play again if there's time.

Older children may enjoy a slight variation to the game. After returning with a card, have them name things that begin with that letter. For example, for the letter "s," children might name snow, stickers, or sunshine.

Keep letter cards in a large envelope, and pull them out often. Add new cards when children demonstrate they know the first batch. Review letters learned on a regular basis to keep recognition from fading.

Pass the Socks, Please!

Creative

Developmental Skill:
Your child will learn large MOTOR SKILLS.

Simple Supplies:
You'll need several pairs of socks.

Make sock "balls" from rolled pairs of socks. You'll want at least three sock balls.

Have children get on their hands and knees, side by side in a line. Explain that you'll play a game passing socks in some very silly ways, and the first way will be passing the socks with their backs. Place a sock ball on the backs of the children on either end of the line. Have them wriggle and wiggle to pass the sock balls to children beside them. You may need to offer a helping hand! Continue until each child has passed a ball on his or her back.

Play Pointer

Young children like "seeing what they can do." Even games with "silly" actions serve a solid purpose—they help children discover new ways to move their bodies and muscles.

Then have children stand where they are and pass sock balls under their legs down the line and back. Use two balls for extra fun. Challenge children to think up new ways to pass the sock balls down a line or around a circle. Then try one or more of the following suggestions.

● Form a circle, and have children pass three sock balls under their chins.

● Form two smaller circles, and have children pass sock balls with elbows, then knees.

● Have children form three lines. Hand the first person in each line a sock ball. Tell children they must use their feet to gently roll the ball to the other end of the room, then back. Have children sit down after their turns, then the next person in line can go. Continue until all children are seated.

● Form a circle sitting down, and use three sock balls to play Hot Potato. Older children will enjoy calling out colors of socks as they roll the ball.

● Let children roll the sock balls at plastic tumblers for a game of Sock-It-to-Me Bowling or toss socks into a Hula Hoop a few feet away.

Quicksand

Discovery

Developmental Skill:
Your child will learn about NATURE.

Simple Supplies:
You'll need spoons, sieves, plastic cups, tubs of sand, and a pitcher of water. You'll also need an old shower curtain.

Spread an old shower curtain on the floor or go outside for this discovery activity. Place two or three tubs of sand on the shower curtain, and set the pitcher beside them. Place spoons, cups, and sieves in the tubs, and let children play in the dry sand. Encourage them to tell how the dry sand feels and how it scoops and pours.

Then begin to add water to the sand. Have children explore how the sand changes in appearance, texture, and "pourability." Continue adding water until the sand is the consistency of quicksand or grainy mud. See if children can scoop the "quicksand" with their fingers and make designs in it. Ask children to tell if the sand is heavier wet or dry and why.

If you're a bit more daring and want to make a "solid" memory, mix several cups of powdered plaster of Paris with the quicksand. (Plaster of Paris is available at most craft stores.) Then immediately scoop the quicksand onto a small *plastic* plate for each child. Let children poke pebbles, small twigs, and leaves on top and partially into the quicksand. As children work, remind them that God made everything in nature including sand, pebbles, leaves, and flowers.

Rinse out the sand tubs with water. The quicksand mixture will thicken and harden within fifteen or twenty minutes. Then pop the hardened quicksand out of the plates. Let children take the creations home to remember their fun discovery time.

Great Grid Game

Spatial

Developmental Skill:
Your child will learn about DIRECTIONS.

Simple Supplies:
You'll need masking tape.

Make a grid on the floor using masking tape. Place six six-foot lines going horizontally and six lines going vertically. Make the lines a foot apart to form twenty-five squares.

Help children "count" off by the letters A, B, and C. Each child should be either an A, a B, or a C. To help children remember which letters they are, write the letters on index cards, and tape a card to each child's shirt.

Play Pointer

This game activity is loads of fun and adds a "thinking" challenge to playtime. Games of skill and creativity are fun, but games fostering cognitive thinking can be just as delightful.

Have children choose squares to stand in. Say: **Look at all the squares on the floor. Today we're going to use those squares to take pretend trips. I'll call out a direction like "B's, go one space forward." Then all the B's will move to the square in front of them. If there isn't an empty square in front of you, move to the closest empty square. We'll see how far everyone can travel.**

Give the following set of directions, and pause for children to travel after each direction.

- **A's, travel two squares backward.**
- **C's, travel one square to the side.**
- **B's, travel one square forward.**
- **A's, travel one square to the side, then one square backward.**
- **C's, travel one square forward, then one square to the side.**
- **B's, travel two squares backward, then one square to the side.**

If children are older, call out two letters at one time, such as "A's and B's travel one square backward." Older children will also enjoy taking turns calling out directions.

End the game by saying: **A's, B's, and C's sit down in your squares.**

Right Hand, Left Hand

Spatial

Developmental Skill:
Your child will learn RIGHT AND LEFT.

Simple Supplies:
You'll need scissors, tape, a marker, and red and yellow construction paper.

Before class, cut out a pair of colorful paper mittens for each child and one for you. Use yellow for the left-hand mittens and red for the right-hand mittens. On the back of each left-hand mitten, write a big letter "L." On the back of each right-hand mitten, write a big letter "R." Be sure that the letters will show when the mittens are placed on the backs of the children's hands.

Tape a yellow mitten on your left hand and a red mitten on your right hand. Be sure the letters show. Say: **God has given us two hands. One is called the left hand** (hold up your left hand, and show the yellow mitten with the letter "L"), **and the other is called the right hand.** Hold up your right hand, and show the red mitten with the letter "R."

Continue: **The letter "L" on my mitten is for the word "left." If you hold your left hand as if you're wearing a mitten, you can make the letter L.** Remove the paper mitten on your left hand. Then stand with your back to the children, and hold up your left hand as if you're wearing a mitten. Show how the thumb makes the bottom part of an L, and the first finger makes the side of an L. Encourage children to make their left hands into letter L's.

Replace the paper mitten on your left hand. Say: **The color of the left mitten is lemon yellow. Here's my right hand.** Hold up your right hand. **The letter "R" on my mitten is for the word "right." And the color is really red.**

Let's play a game with our left and right hands. First, you'll need some pretty mittens like mine! Tape paper mittens to the backs of the children's hands. Be sure the letters are showing. Then have them hold up their left hands and right hands. When children feel comfortable with "right" and "left," begin the following game.

Say: **Let's play a fun game with our left and right hands. Listen to the directions! Ready? Right hand, touch your nose.** Pause for children to touch their noses with their red mittens. Then say: **Good! Now left hand, touch your toes.** Pause for children to respond with their yellow mittens. Continue giving more right hand-left hand directions. Then make the game more challenging by giving directions such as "Right hand, touch your left ear" and "Left hand, tickle you right foot."

When you're finished, try one or more of these right hand-left hand variations.

● Have children get with partners for a clapping game. Have children clap right hands together, then left hands. Let children call out "right" or "left" directions for clapping.

● Remove the paper mittens, and play the right hand-left hand game. To start, tell children each to put on a pretend mitten to find which hand makes the letter L for the left hand.

● Tape the paper mittens to the children's right and left feet, and give directions for a game of Footsy.

Square Switch

Spatial

Developmental Skill:
Your child will learn NUMBER RECOGNITION.

Simple Supplies:
You'll need masking tape, index cards, and a marker.

Make number cards by writing numerals from zero through five on index cards. Put one numeral on each card. Make sure there's a card for each child in class and one complete set for yourself. You need to have at least two children with the same number. If your class is smaller than twelve, use only numbers one, two, and three. Stick a five-foot masking tape square on the floor.

Tape a number card to the back of each child's hand. Have all the Zeros raise their hands, all the Ones raise their hands, and so on until each child knows what number he or she is. Tell children to remember their numbers. Then help them find a place to stand around the square. Arrange children so that those with the matching numbers are on opposite sides of the square.

Play Pointer

Use "Bible numbers" to help kids learn number recognition. Bible numbers include:
● 1 (God)
● 7 (days of Creation)
● 2 (animals by pairs to the ark)
● 3 (days Jonah spent in fish)

Explain that when you call out a number, children with that number exchange places. For example, if you hold up and call out the number four, all the Fours would exchange places. Continue calling numbers until each child has changed places three times. Then try calling two numbers simultaneously. You may wish to direct the way children move to exchange places, such as walking, hopping, crawling, or tiptoeing.

For a twist, play silently. Don't call out the number, simply hold up a number card. For more fun variations, try one of the following suggestions.

● Have children arrange themselves in numerical order. You'll need to make two or more lines, depending on your class size. Then have children count out loud.

● Let children tape the number cards on their shirts. Then have them mill around the room until you call out, "Number pair-up." Have children each find someone wearing the same number card and give them a high five. Then have children mill again.

● Have children play dominoes with the number cards. Start the game by placing one of your cards on the floor, and letting children with that same number place their cards beside it. Then put down another number card. Continue laying down cards until all the cards have been used.

Travel Box Costumes

Creative

Developmental Skill:
Your child will learn about IMAGINATION.

Simple Supplies:
You'll need washable markers, tape, paper plates, crepe paper, scissors, and construction paper. You'll also need a medium-sized box for each child. Remove all flaps and bottoms from the boxes so they're four-sided squares.

Gather children and ask: **What are different ways to travel?** Encourage children to name ways, such as by car, boat, airplane, wagon, and train. Then say: **Today we'll make travel boxes to wear as costumes. You can choose what you want your box to be. It can be an airplane, a tractor, a bus, a fire truck, a car, or a boat. We'll make our costumes from these boxes. You can add color and cutouts and make them any way you'd like. Then we'll tape on paper plate steering wheels so we can go for rides.**

Hand each child a medium-sized box. Let children decorate their pretend vehicles with markers or crayons and construction paper. Tape a paper-plate steering wheel in each vehicle. Cut two three-foot lengths of crepe paper for each child. Securely tape or staple two crepe paper strips to each box in a crisscross fashion to make shoulder straps. These will hold the boxes in place on the children's shoulders. (See illustration.)

When all the fantasy vehicles are finished, invite children to put on their costumes and go for a ride around the room. Play lively music for a zippy touch. Then ask children where they'd like to go on a special "trip." Suggest places such as the moon, Africa, or Nursery Rhyme Land. Make up sights you'd see along the way and people or friendly animals you'd meet.

Send the imaginative crafts home with the children to keep fun "on the go" all week long.

Yo-Ho!

Conversational

Developmental Skill:
Your child will learn EXPRESSION.

Simple Supplies:
You'll need cardboard tubes, stickers, and washable markers. Empty bathroom tissue tubes or portions of paper towel tubes work well for this activity.

Hand children each a cardboard tube, and invite them to decorate the tubes using markers and stickers. As children work, explain that they're making "spy tubes" to peek at things around the room. Work alongside children and make a spy tube of your own.

When the spy tubes are complete, gather children in a group on the floor. Peek through your spy tube at something in the room. For example, if you spy an apple, say, "Yo-ho! I see something that's red and delicious to eat. What do I see?" Children can then answer "apple" and use their spy tubes to peek at the apple.

Play Pointer

Encouraging young children to describe what they see, hear, and smell in sensory terms helps them share their emotions more freely.

You can also peek at children through the tube and describe them. For example, you can say, "Yo-ho! I see someone who has brown hair and pretty eyes. She's wearing a pink dress. Who do I see?" Then let children identify the child by looking through their tubes and telling her name. Then invite someone else to have a turn peeking through his or her tube and describing what's seen. Have children begin their descriptions by saying, "Yo-ho! I see..." Let the other children guess what or who is sighted.

Use one or more of the following suggestions for extra activities.

● Let children spy other children's smiles and affirm their friends by saying, "(Child's name) has a happy smile."

● Place the tubes at one end of the room. Have children hop to find their tubes, then look through their tubes as they walk back to their starting places.

● Lead children in the following action rhyme. Have them look around the room and at their friends as they repeat the words.

Yo-ho, yo-ho,
Look what I see.
God's bright world,
A bright big smile,
Happy friends and me!

Foiled Again

Discovery

Developmental Skill:
Your child will learn about HANDS.

Simple Supplies:
You'll need heavy-duty aluminum foil, clear tape, and fishing line. Tear off one twelve-inch piece of heavy-duty aluminum foil for each child.

Have children get into pairs. Say: **I have a riddle for you. Hold up your hand when you know what I'm describing.**
I pick things up off the ground.
I'm really *handy* to have around.
What am I?

Help children discover that you're describing hands. Tell partners to place their hands beside each other's hands and take a careful look. Ask children the following discovery questions about hands.

● **How are hands alike? different?**
● **How many fingers are on each hand?**
● **How many fingernails?**
● **Are all fingers the same length?**
● **What are hands used for?**

Say: **God gave us hands. Hands and fingers are very special. They help us pick things up. They help us write and draw. They help us eat and point to things. And hands help us serve God and work for him. Let's take pictures of our special hands and fingers in a fun new way. I'll hand each of you a piece of shiny foil.**

Demonstrate the following directions as you talk. **Place your hand flat on the floor, and spread your fingers as wide as they'll go. Then have your partner place a piece of foil over your hand and gently push the foil around your hand and between your fingers.** Place foil over your hand and mold it around your fingers. **Then carefully lift off the foil, and you'll have a perfect picture of your very own special hand!** Hold up the foil mold of your hand.

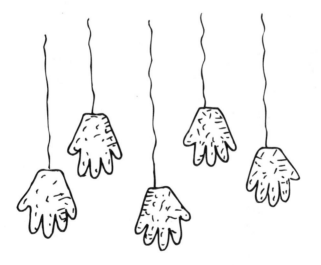

Hand each child a piece of foil. Circulate and offer help as needed. When all the hands are finished, tape a two-foot piece of fishing line to the top of each one, and suspend the line from the ceiling. You may wish to tape a small slip of paper with the children's names on the foil hand prints.

Group Game

Conversational

Developmental Skill:

Your child will learn about GROUPS.

Simple Supplies:

You'll need one or two beanbags. Make instant beanbags by pouring uncooked beans or rice into socks, then securely knotting the ankles and cutting off excess fabric.

Have children form two lines facing each other, about three feet apart. Say: **Some things belong to certain groups such as colors or foods. We can play an exciting game about groups. The first group we'll name are colors.**

Ask: **What are some different colors?** Pause for response.

Say: **When I start the game, we'll toss beanbags back and forth, up and down the lines. When you catch a beanbag, tell the name of a color. It's OK if you name a color someone else has named, but be sure you name a color.**

Play Pointer

Keep naming games simple and unhurried. Children need time to think and reason before giving answers, so discourage time limits or "peer-pushing."

Begin the game by tossing a beanbag. Give each child all the time he or she needs to name a color. Then have the child toss the beanbag to the person across from him or her. Have that child name a color and toss the beanbag.

After everyone has caught the beanbag and named a color, have children at the end of the line start the beanbag back and forth as they name kinds of food. Other groups to name might include

- animals,
- boys' and girls' names,
- alphabet letters,
- types of toys, and
- furniture in a house.

Older children might even enjoy the challenge of naming words that rhyme with "cat" or things that begin with certain letter sounds.

Who's That Angel?

Conversational

Developmental Skill:
Your child will learn OBSERVATION.

Simple Supplies:
You'll need a bedsheet.

Gather children in a group. Say: **Look around the room. What do you see?** Let children tell what they observe. Then ask children to look at their friends and tell what they see. Encourage children to tell the name of each child in class. Then say: **Let's play a guessing game to see how well you notice who's here and who's missing. I'll ask you to hide your eyes. Then I'll tap someone to come put this pretend angel robe on so he or she is all covered up.**

Hold up the bedsheet—or put it over your head. Say: **You can spread out your arms like wings to make yourself like a big angel or stand on tiptoe to look like a tall angel or scrunch way down to look like a very little angel. Then I'll say, "Open your eyes—what a surprise! Who is the angel before your eyes?"** And you can guess who the angel is.

> ### Play Pointer
> Observation is a good skill for young children to learn, and games of guessing what or who is missing help make children keen observers.

Have children hide their eyes, then tap someone to be the angel. Continue playing until each child has had a turn hiding under the sheet. For a twist, choose two people to hide under the sheet and be "twin" angels. Let children guess the names of both angels.

Remind children that God sends angels to love, help, and protect us. End with a brief prayer thanking God for his loving angels.

In Great Shape

Spatial

Developmental Skill:
Your child will learn about SHAPES.

Simple Supplies:
You'll need pairs of construction paper shapes, such as triangles, circles,

squares, hearts, stars, and rectangles. You'll need a pair of shapes for every child.

Gather children in a group. Scatter the paper shapes on the floor in front of you. Hold up one of the paper shapes and ask: **What shape is this? Can you find a matching shape on the floor?** Have children take turns identifying and finding the shapes.

Then say: **I'm going to hand each of you a shape. Keep it secret! Then when I say, "Go match," find the person with the shape that matches yours. When you find your match, sit down and hold up your shape.**

When all children are seated, say: **Good for you! Now exchange shapes with someone and tell that person the kind of shape you have. Then we'll play Go Match again.**

After you've played Go Match several times, have children hold their shapes and sit in a large circle. Make sure no one is sitting by someone who is holding the same shape.

Say: **I'll say the name of a shape. If you're holding that shape, stand up and switch places with someone else who has the same shape. We'll see how many times you can move around the circle. Ready? Circles, stand up!** Have children with circle shapes exchange places, then call another shape. Continue until you've called each shape at least two times.

Try one of these variations to help reinforce shape identification.

● Pass shapes around the circle until you say "stop." Then children holding the heart shapes must identify the shapes on either side of them.

● Let half the children hide their shapes, then have the remaining half hunt for the shapes that match the ones they're holding. Then switch "hiders" and "hunters."

Wall Dominoes

Conversational

Developmental Skill:
Your child will learn LETTER SOUNDS.

Simple Supplies:
You'll need index cards, sticky tack or tape, markers, and a large envelope.

Before class, make a double set of alphabet cards by writing a letter on each index card.

Gather children by a blank wall. Scatter one set of alphabet cards on the floor, but hold the other set. Say: **Let's sing the "Alphabet Song." Who would like to start us?** Have a child start the "Alphabet Song" and sing it through a couple of times.

Then say: **We can play an unusual game of dominoes. Instead of playing on the floor, we'll play on the wall! We'll tape up letter cards, then think of things that begin with that letter. I'll help you, and we'll work together to get all the way through the alphabet. Now who can find the letter "A"?**

Hold up your letter "A" card for a clue. Choose a child to find the letter card and attach it to the wall using sticky tack or tape. Then encourage children to name things that begin with the letter A such as "apple," "alligator," and "apron." Children will need considerable help with vowels as beginning sounds.

Play Pointer

Letter sounds and their identification encourage and motivate children to verbalize words and sounds—and begin reading simple words even at a young age. The best part? Letter games make learning a snap!

When all the alphabet letters are on the wall, sing the "Alphabet Song" again and point to the letters as you sing. Sing the song a couple of times. If there's time, let children match pairs with the letter cards. Keep the letter cards in a labeled envelope and review letters and sounds often to keep learning fresh.

Here's a fun variation:

● Let children point to the letters that begin the following words: "God," "Bible," "love," "Jesus," "forgive," and "pray."

Roller Racers

Discovery

Developmental Skill:
Your child will learn about SPEED.

Simple Supplies:
You'll need a golf ball and a twelve-inch-by-four-foot cardboard "ramp" for each pair of children.

Have children form pairs, and hand each pair a golf ball and a cardboard or poster board "ramp." Say: **Today we'll learn about rolling balls and what makes them roll fast. Decide which partner will be the first Roller and who will be the first Holder.**

The Holder will hold the ramp flat on the floor, and the Roller can place the ball on the cardboard to see if it rolls. Then the Holder can raise the ramp a bit, and the Roller can let the ball go down the ramp. Keep making the ramp steeper and steeper and see how fast the ball rolls. Then we'll switch Holders and Rollers and try again.

Let partners experiment with ramp angles to see how it affects the speed of the rolling ball. After several moments, have Holders and Rollers switch roles. When you're finished, have children place the golf balls on the ramps and have children tell what they discovered. Help them realize that the steeper the ramp, the faster the ball rolls.

End with a just-for-fun game. Let partners sit several feet apart and roll the golf balls back and forth. Place blocks in front of partners to "bowl" over.

Bingo-Bongo!

Spatial

Developmental Skill:
Your child will learn COLORS AND SHAPES.

Simple Supplies:
You'll need crayons, cereal loops, and photocopies of the game board on page 88.

Hand each child a photocopy of "Bingo-Bongo!" from page 88. Have children color the squares red, the circles yellow, the stars green, and the rectangles purple.

Play Pointer

Young children love bingo games—but don't feel as if you need to offer prizes for winning. In Bingo-Bongo! everyone wins at once—and community fun is the best prize of all!

Hand each child a handful of cereal loops to use as game markers. Then play the game like bingo. Explain that when children have covered all the pictures with cereal loops, they can shout, "Bingo-Bongo!" Call out colors and shapes, and have children place cereal loops on the correct pictures. For example, call out, "Red square." Each time a child sees a red square, have him or her place a cereal loop on that picture. Won't all the children shout, "Bingo-Bongo!" at once? Yes! That's the cooperative fun!

Have children end the game by snacking on their game pieces!

Here are other suggestions for twists on this classic game.

● Have older children cover only one shape at a time and play until someone has five cereal loops in a row.

● Have children play until only the four corners are covered or make another simple configuration such as a cross or the squares on the edges.

● Let children take turns calling out colors or shapes—not both simultaneously.

● Before photocopying, write numbers or letters on each shape then play Bingo-Bongo! by calling out alphabet letters or numbers.

Sam Went to Sleep

Creative

Developmental Skill:
Your child will learn IMITATION.

Simple Supplies:
none

Have children form a circle. Say: **I know a silly game we can play. It's called Sam Went to Sleep. I'll begin by saying, "Sam went to sleep like this** (add a funny action such as patting your head)**." Then all of you can imitate what I do. Pat your heads. Now keep patting them while I say, "Sam went to sleep like this** (keep patting your head, and hop up and down)**." That's right, hop up and down and keep patting your head as you hop. Now I'll add another. "Sam went to sleep like this** (pat your head, hop, and open and close your eyes)**."**

Encourage children to follow all your silly directions. When everyone is confused and giggling, begin again. Limit yourself to three or four motions to avoid frustration—both yours and the children's!

Older children will enjoy giving their own versions of how Sam went to sleep. Or use one of the silly sentences below to give the game new life.

● Davie milked the cow like this...
● Daddy washed the car like this...
● The puppy chased his tail like this...
● The man walked on the moon like this...

Surprise Packages

Creative

Developmental Skill:
Your child will learn about the element of SURPRISE.

Simple Supplies:
You'll need letter envelopes, a paper grocery sack, crayons, tape, and a variety of small tactile items including pennies, leaves, sandpaper shapes, nickels, and uncooked rice.

Before this activity, place two or three of the tactile items in each envelope, then lick and stick it closed. Prepare three or four "surprise packages" for each child. Place the packages in a paper grocery sack.

Play Pointer

The element of surprise is a teacher's and parent's best friend. It keeps children motivated, excited, and experiencing their world in fresh new ways.

Gather children at a table, and set out crayons. Let them reach into the paper sack and choose a surprise package. Show children how to use crayons to color over the envelopes to reveal what's inside each package.

Encourage children to use a variety of colors and to experiment with coloring lightly and with more pressure. When the envelopes have been colored, have children tell what was in their packages and then carefully open them to see if they were right.

After children have opened their packages, invite them each to choose another surprise package to reveal. Tape the envelopes closed after each round, and send the envelopes home as pretty craft projects.

If children seem to enjoy this activity, create a coloring center complete with white paper, crayons, and a tub of tactile items to slip under the paper and color over. Challenge children to see how many prints they can collect.

Happy Hopscotch

Spatial

Developmental Skill:
Your child will learn about large MOTOR SKILLS.

Simple Supplies:
You'll need an old shower curtain, permanent markers, masking tape, and beanbags.

This game is a boon for rainy days and is as portable as any game board. But before playing, you need to prepare the hopscotch board by drawing two game outlines on the back of an old shower curtain. Use the illustration to guide you. Color each square a different color—include red, yellow, green, blue, and orange squares. Draw letters and numbers with a black marker.

Play Pointer

Old fashioned games get a new lease on life when you make them portable, colorful, and "larger than life." Other great games that lend themselves to old shower curtains are four-square, checkers, bingo, and large target-toss games.

When the hopscotch mat is ready, tape it to the floor with masking tape or clear packing tape. Place a beanbag by each game outline. Have children form two groups. Have each group line up by one of the games. Decide if you want children to identify the colors, the letters, or the numbers on which the beanbags land. Then have each child toss a beanbag, call out the letter, the number, or the color and hop through the game. Or children may play the game without tossing beanbags—simply hop and enjoy the exercise! You can add lively background music for festive fun. You can also review the story of Noah's ark, then invite children to play hopscotch on a rainbow.

After several rounds of hopping, have groups switch letter and number games. When you're finished playing, either leave the hopscotch mat in place or fold it up for another day of rainy day hoppity play.

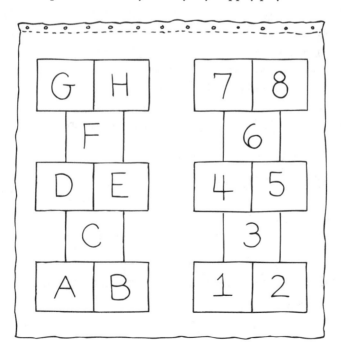

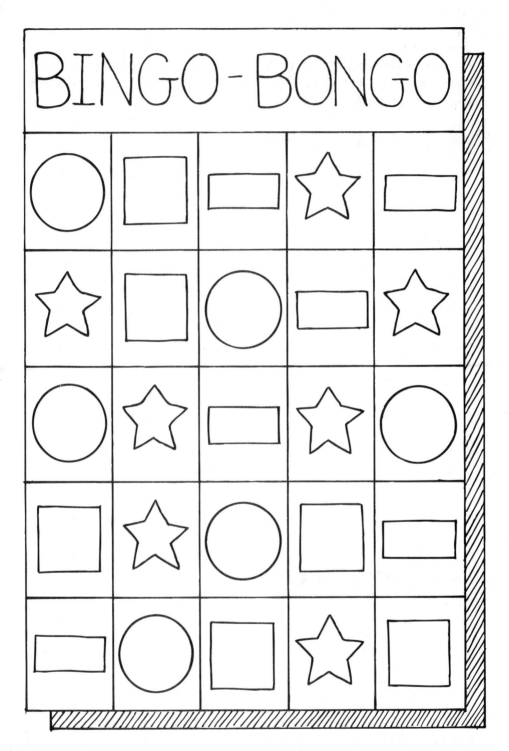

Game Guide

Since games and activities rarely fit solely into one play type, the chart below reflects the major emphasis (✱ ✱) and secondary emphasis (✱) of each game and activity included in *Age-Right Play.*

Title of game or activity	CREATIVE	SPATIAL	DISCOVERY	CONVERSATIONAL
Personal and Parallel Play				
Box Walk (p. 32)	✱ ✱		✱	
Bunny in the House (p. 20)	✱ ✱			✱
Cereal Sorter (p. 17)		✱ ✱	✱	
Clackety Cups (p. 17)	✱	✱ ✱		
Copycat Ring-a-Ding (p. 30)	✱ ✱			✱
Glad Doggie, Sad Doggie (p. 15)	✱			✱ ✱
I See a Cat (p. 29)	✱ ✱			✱
In and Out of the Mountains (p. 26)	✱	✱ ✱		
Leader of the Band Batons (p. 33)	✱ ✱			✱
Little Echo (p. 30)	✱			✱ ✱
Little Fishy (p. 25)	✱	✱ ✱		
Mirror, Mirror (p. 16)	✱		✱ ✱	
One, Two, Peekaboo! (p. 18)		✱ ✱		✱
Oopsie-Dropsie (p. 23)		✱ ✱	✱	
Picture Bags (p. 31)		✱ ✱	✱	
Pretty Petunia (p. 28)			✱ ✱	✱
Picture Boxes (p. 26)		✱		✱ ✱
Pudding Painting (p. 24)	✱ ✱		✱	
Roly-Ball (p. 21)		✱ ✱	✱	
Rum-Sum-Sum (p. 22)	✱ ✱			✱
Shape Collage (p. 27)	✱	✱ ✱		
Surprise Purse (p. 19)	✱			✱ ✱
Terry Tooth (p. 34)			✱ ✱	✱
What's That? (p. 21)	✱			✱ ✱
Partner Play				
Balancing Game (p. 60)		✱	✱ ✱	
Bedtime Puppies (p. 52)		✱		✱ ✱
Bowl Me Over (p. 37)		✱ ✱	✱	
Burger Shop (p. 55)	✱ ✱			✱
Dough Duos (p. 51)		✱	✱ ✱	
Fruit Matchups (p. 57)	✱	✱ ✱		
Hanging Out Together (p. 52)		✱		✱ ✱
Hop Like a Froggy (p. 44)	✱ ✱			✱
Love Those Leaves (p. 45)	✱		✱ ✱	

Title of game or activity	CREATIVE	SPATIAL	DISCOVERY	CONVERSATIONAL
Match Me! (p. 47)		✳ ✳		✳
Moving Day (p. 40)		✳ ✳	✳	
Oceans of Fun (p. 50)		✳	✳ ✳	
Partner Books (p. 39)	✳ ✳			✳
Partner Pizzas (p. 42)		✳ ✳	✳	
Picture Packs (p. 38)	✳			✳ ✳
Potato Patch (p. 46)			✳	✳ ✳
Rainbows (p. 43)		✳	✳ ✳	
Roads 'n' Rides (p. 55)	✳ ✳	✳		
Row Your Boat (p. 60)	✳			✳ ✳
Silly Stories (p. 56)	✳			✳ ✳
Snowball Catch (p. 49)	✳	✳ ✳		
Steppingstones (p. 42)	✳	✳ ✳		
The Chicken and the Egg (p. 40)	✳			✳ ✳
Tiger Tail (p. 48)	✳ ✳			✳
Twin Turtles (p. 59)	✳ ✳			✳

Peer Play

Bingo-Bongo! (p. 84)	✳	✳ ✳		
Cooperative Banner (p. 66)	✳ ✳	✳		
Foiled Again (p. 78)	✳		✳ ✳	
Great Grid Game (p. 72)		✳ ✳	✳	
Group Game (p. 80)		✳		✳ ✳
Guard the Gorilla (p. 65)		✳		✳ ✳
Happy Hopscotch (p. 86)	✳	✳ ✳		
In Great Shape (p. 81)	✳	✳ ✳		
Kangaroo Romp (p. 68)	✳ ✳			✳
Letter Snatch (p. 69)		✳		✳ ✳
Pass the Socks, Please! (p. 70)	✳ ✳			✳
Quicksand (p. 71)	✳		✳ ✳	
Right Hand, Left Hand (p. 73)		✳ ✳	✳	
Roller Racers (p. 83)		✳	✳ ✳	
Sam Went to Sleep (p. 85)	✳ ✳			✳
Small, Medium, Large (p. 67)		✳	✳ ✳	
Square Switch (p. 75)		✳ ✳		✳
Surprise Packages (p. 86)	✳ ✳		✳	
Travel Box Costumes (p. 76)	✳ ✳			✳
Wall Dominoes (p. 82)	✳			✳ ✳
Who's That Angel? (p. 81)			✳	✳ ✳
Yo-Ho! (p. 77)	✳			✳ ✳

Group Publishing, Inc.
Attention: Books & Curriculum
P.O. Box 481
Loveland, CO 80539
Fax: (970) 669-1994

Evaluation for *AGE-RIGHT PLAY*

Please help Group Publishing, Inc., continue to provide innovative and useful resources for ministry. Please take a moment to fill out this evaluation and mail or fax it to us. Thanks!

● ● ●

1. As a whole, this book has been (circle one):

Not very helpful   Very helpful

1   2   3   4   5   6   7   8   9   10

2. The best things about this book:

3. Ways this book could be improved:

4. Things I will change because of this book:

5. Other books I'd like to see Group publish in the future:

6. Would you be interested in field-testing future Group products and giving us your feedback? If so, please fill in the information below:

Name _____

Street Address _____

City _____ State _____ Zip _____

Phone Number _____ Date_____

Four Read-Aloud Stories That Unfold Before Your Children's Eyes!

Each **Foldover Bible Story** invites your children to help solve a problem...

- *Do You See the Star?* follows a shepherd as he searches for a distant glow.
  ISBN 1-55945-617-5

- *Jesus, What's for Lunch?* considers a favorite Bible story from the viewpoint of a child who is way past lunch time.
  ISBN 1-55945-620-5

- In *Little Lamb, Where Did You Go?* children join a young shepherd in looking high and low for a lost lamb.
  ISBN 1-55945-618-3

- In *Noah, Noah, What'll We Do?* Noah needs help sorting out mixed-up animals.
  ISBN 1-55945-619-1

Lively, rhyming text and vivid illustrations hint at possible solutions, so even your youngest children will offer suggestions as the story unfolds. But not until the very last panel is everything clear!

Order all four **Foldover Bible Story** books *now* and delight children in Sunday school...children's church...preschool...at home...*anywhere* children love to snuggle up to a good story!

Order today from your local Christian bookstore, or write: Group Publishing, P.O. Box 485, Loveland, CO 80539.

TEACH YOUR PRESCHOOLERS AS JESUS TAUGHT WITH GROUP'S HANDS-ON BIBLE CURRICULUM™

Hands-On Bible Curriculum™ for preschoolers helps your preschoolers learn the way they learn best—by touching, exploring, and discovering. With active learning, preschoolers love learning about the Bible, and they really remember what they learn.

Because small children learn best through repetition, Preschoolers and Pre-K & K will learn one important point per lesson, and Toddlers & 2s will learn one point each month with **Hands-On Bible Curriculum**. These important lessons will stick with them and comfort them during their daily lives. Your children will learn:

•God is our friend,
•who Jesus is, and
•we can always trust Jesus.

The **Learning Lab®** is packed with age-appropriate learning tools for fun, faith-building lessons. Toddlers & 2s explore big **Interactive StoryBoards™** with enticing textures that toddlers love to touch—like sandpaper for earth, cotton for clouds, and blue cellophane for water. **Bible Big Books™** captivate Preschoolers and Pre-K & K while teaching them important Bible lessons. With **Jumbo Bible Puzzles™** and involving **Learning Mats™**, your children will see, touch, and explore their Bible stories. Each quarter there's a brand new collection of supplies to keep your lessons fresh and involving.

Fuzzy, age-appropriate hand puppets are also available to add to the learning experience. These child-friendly puppets help you teach each lesson with scripts provided in the **Teachers Guide**. Plus, your children will enjoy teaching the puppets what they learn. Cuddles the Lamb, Whiskers the Mouse, and Pockets the Kangaroo turn each lesson into an interactive and entertaining learning experience.

Just order one **Learning Lab** and one **Teachers Guide** for each age level, add a few common classroom supplies, and presto—you have everything you need to build faith in your children. For more interactive fun, introduce your children to the age-appropriate puppet who will be your teaching assistant and their friend. **No student books are required!**

Hands-On Bible Curriculum is also available for grades 1–6.

MORE PRACTICAL RESOURCES
FOR YOUR MINISTRY TO PRESCHOOLERS

Saving Your Sanity: A Creative System for Teaching Preschoolers
Susan L. Lingo

With just 4 ordinary cardboard boxes and a small supply of simple, everyday items, you'll keep your class of preschoolers laughing and learning week after week. You get dozens of attention-grabbing **activities**...creative, no-mess **crafts**...super **stories and songs**...and sanity-saving **secrets**! All with easy-to-follow directions. And all you'll need are those 4 boxes from the basement...some odds and ends...and this book, of course.

ISBN 0-7644-2027-5

Preschool Craft-Play

Discover over 100 just-for-fun creative crafts for preschool-age children. Each craft is simple to make and fun to play with and encourages creative expression in children. Included: craft ideas for each month of the year, special events, and holidays.

ISBN 1-55945-610-8

First & Favorite Bible Lessons for Preschoolers
Beth Rowland Wolf & Bonnie Temple

The 13 *"most important* Bible stories preschoolers can learn!" That's what a national survey of preschool teachers told us, and now you'll easily share these lessons with *your* children. Lessons, games, drama, songs, and snacks all reinforce these foundational Bible truths. For children's church leaders, Christian day-care providers, Christian school teachers, and parents.

ISBN 1-55945-614-0

"Let's Play!" Group Games for Preschoolers

You'll make playtime *learning* time with exciting games that work in any size class! These 140 easy-to-lead, fun-to-play games teach preschoolers about Bible characters and stories. And because directions are simple and clear, you'll see "I can do it!" smiles on your children's faces as they enjoy these games again and again! Now you'll have just the right game at just the right time—in Sunday school...children's church...in preschool...and *anywhere* preschoolers want to play!

ISBN 1-55945-613-2